The Abstract Arsenal of
Zen
and the
Psychology of Being

```
Further Zen Ramblings from the Internet
```

Scott Shaw

Buddha Rose Publication

The Abstract Arsenal of Zen
and the Psychology of Being
Further Zen Ramblings from the Internet

Copyright © 2016 by Scott Shaw
www.scottshaw.com

Rear cover photograph of Scott Shaw
by Hae Won Shin Copyright © 2016

No Part of this book may be reproduced in any manner without the expressed written permission of the publishing company.

First Edition 2016

ISBN: 1-877792-91-8
ISBN 13: 9781877792915

Library of Congress Control Number: 2016947595

Printed in the United States of America

10 9 8 7 6 5 4 3 2 1

The Abstract Arsenal of Zen and the Psychology of Being

Introduction

Life is about consciousness. Life is about consciously living. The more consciously you live your life the more refined understanding you develop about the inner-workings of yourself, human kind, the universe, and god.

Most people spend their entire lifetime driven by unchecked emotions and desires. They run from wanting to anger about not getting. When they do get they are happy for a moment but then they want something more and they are no longer happy. Thus, they are again driven to disharmony and rage about not having all that they desire. Though this is a common thread that runs through the life of many/most people, this is the ideal example of a life defined by lack of consciousness — as there is nothing conscious about desire, wanting, and rage.

Everyone wants what they want. This is an element of the human condition. This being said, the conscious individual, (the person who walks the path of consciousness), does not let desire(s) and/or emotion(s) control their actions and reactions to the world around us — for they understand if a person does this they believe themselves to be the center of this universe; which they are not. Many people who falsely believe themselves to be the most important thing in this *lifescape* do whatever they deem necessary to get what they want and, by living life in this manner, they injure the lives of all those around them. This is never the path of consciousness.

Many people are falsely feed the belief that if they ask for forgiveness, if they do something good, then their wrongs are righted. No, this is incorrect. Yes, at some point an individual who has wronged others, driven by their own emotions and desires, may feel sorry for their actions, but the only doing worth doing, the only source for forgiveness is the undoing of anything bad you have done. But, this is virtually impossible in this Life Space. What you have done is what you have done and though you may seek forgiveness for your actions — your asking forgiveness from a religious elder or some divine entity never can change what you have done. Thus, the person, persons, or Life Space you have damaged, remains damaged.

People wanting something/anything gives birth to lying. People wanting, gives birth to damaging actions. People wanting, gives birth to bad behavior. People wanting, never gives birth to refined consciousness.

The fact is, in this world, people seek. They seek possessions, they seek position, they seek power, some even seek enlightenment. But, the common factor, and the incorrect element to this equation is, *"The seeking."* For at the very root of seeking arises the desire for things to be different than they already are. At the very root of seeking is born the concept of unhappiness due to not having. From this, all the damage to others, all the damage to the earth, all the damage to the all and the everything is given birth to.

At the root of Life Betterment is consciousness — focused human consciousness. As humans, all we can be is humans. As humans, we are defined by being human. This being said, it is the person who chooses the path of refining their consciousness that <u>consciously</u> eliminates as many of the negative obstacles of human existence as possible; namely: uncontrolled desire, equaling rage, equaling lying, equaling power-grabbing and power-tripping. From this, the damage unleashed onto others is minimalized and the world becomes just a slightly better place.

In this pages of this book life, life occurrences, and life actions and reactions will be detailed and discussed. From this, each of you who reads these words may be able to learn from experiences that you did not have to personally live through but were able to study those experiences lived by the life of others. From this, new understandings of a better way to live life and react to life may be understood. Thus, a more conscious world may be born where you, personally, may have the chance to become a more wholly fulfilled and conscious *Live-er* in this Life Space.

Foreword

Here it is, *The Scott Shaw Zen Blog 6.0,* originally presented on the World Wide Web. All of the writings presented in this book were written between late March and mid July of 2016 with a few placements from September of 2015.

As was the case with the previously published volumes based upon *The Scott Shaw Zen Blog;* entitled: *Scribbles on the Restroom Wall, The Chronicles: Zen Ramblings from the Internet, Words in the Wind, Zen Mind Life Thoughts, The Zen of Life, Lies, and Aberrant Reality,* and *Apostrophe Zen* this volume is presented exactly as it was viewed on scottshaw.com with no rewriting, punctuation, or typo corrections. From this, we hope you will receive the original reading experience.'

This volume of internet ramblings is presented with the date and time listed as to when each blog was originally posted. Also, the blogs in this volume are presented from last to first. With this, we hope to present a transcendence back through time as opposed to an evolving evolution. In addition, we left out the traditional *Table of Contents* in an attempt to leave this volume with a much more free-flowing reading experience.

Okay, there's the information and the definitions. Read on... We hope you enjoy it. And, be sure to stayed tuned for the ongoing *Scott Shaw Zen Blog* @ scottshaw.com.

The Scott Shaw Zen Blog 6.0

Remembering How to Be Young
10/07/16 08:01

As I spoke about in this blog a while back, my best-bud of a cat recently passed away, way too young. It was heart breaking. As I also mentioned, cats are not solitary creatures — they do not want to be alone. As we have another cat, who kept looking for her lost friend, I decided to get another cat. So, I found a breeder up in the high desert and purchased this spunky little kitten. He's great!

In any case, our older cat was always the more playful of the previous two. My main bud was grumpier and only liked the love of people, whereas she would run around playing with balls and string all the time. I assumed that if we brought a kitten into her life, once they got accustomed to one another, it would be non-stop playtime. But, no. It is not. The kitten plays and she wants nothing to do with him. Now, she sits around doing nothing, just staring at him as he plays.

Sadly, she is not young anymore. At least so she thinks.

How many people do you know that get old way too young? How many people do you know that act old where there is no need to do so? Do you?

Now, life-is-life, we all need to, *"Grow up,"* and make our own way through the world. We all need to find a way to pay our own bills. But, we do not need to become, *"Old,"* in the process. We do not need to freeze out our youth.

For example, have you ever met a person that maybe had a few grey hairs and you knew they had some years under their belt but they were still full of youthful energy, ready to try new things, do fun things, and truly embrace life? They hold onto their youth. …Not in some weird way like those old people who get all inked-up and wear clothing made specifically for the teenager attempting to look young, when they are not. But, instead, those that have remained young on the inside, projecting to the outside.

As you move through life you gain new experiences. The more years under your belt, the more you hopefully will acquire wisdom. You learn what is the best thing(s) to do and what things are better that you do not say or do. This is life. Wisdom through time. But, within this path of ever-gaining wisdom you don't have to act like you know-it-all like some people do, you don't have to separate yourself from the joy of living life, you don't have to become old. You can still embrace being young.

Old or young, which one are you?

What Are You Going to Do When?
09/07/16 20:21

When I was in my early twenties I was at my girlfriend's house and her mother was making us dinner. Her mother looked around her kitchen and said, *"Someday I am going to have a big kitchen."* The mother was in her early fifties and the thought, from my young mind was, *"You better hurry up."*

Life goes by very fast. We when we are young, we only see the future — we believe that there is time and we know that what we want will come to us soon. Soon disintegrates, however. It disintegrates to life, doing what we need to do to survive, making ends meets, and mostly age. There is no universal golden ring, age gets us all and most of us will never even come close to living the life that we have envisioned for ourselves.

Whether it is a relatively small thing like a, *"Big kitchen,"* or greater dreams like I hold, to make the world a better place, it is near-impossible to have and to do all that we hope for. This is the curse of life.

As I look back to that aforementioned moment, with the lady hoping for a bigger kitchen, I could only define her desires by what I had lived; having grown up, for the most part, it pretty dismal circumstances. To me, her kitchen was great. But, to her, she wanted more, she wanted, *"Bigger."*

We all want more. We all want, *"That."* Whatever that, *"That,"* may be. Some of us work towards THAT. But, most of us do not. Most, simply want what they want but they do nothing to achieve. Thus, they hate all those who have achieved. But, that is the wrong attitude. The pathway to achievement is to first develop yourself to the point where you can actually accomplish and then consciously move towards what you hope to accomplish with a precise game plan. But most, never do this: they talk, they criticize, they berate, they create turmoil within and outside of themselves but the never actually DO. Why is this? Because ultimate they can't DO because they do not lay the foundations for their doing. Thus, their life is lost. Most lives are lost because they do not try.

You can desire all you want. You can criticize all those who have achieved all you want. But, if you ever want YOU to be all that YOU want YOU to become you must turn off all levels of negativity, focus, lay out a game place, and try.

*   *   *

08/07/16 20:16

What works, works for a little while but then it doesn't work anymore.

**Tell'n You What's Right
When You Know That It's Wrong**
07/07/16 09:26

Have you ever had the experience when you were talking to someone and they were telling you something as if it was etched-in-stone, factual information, but you knew that what they were saying was totally wrong?

People are belief dominate. People want to be seen as right and all-knowing. But, most people know nothing. They may believe what they believe but what they believe is only that; what they believe. Belief is not fact; it is only belief. Yet, people will fight to their dying day to get you believe what they believe.

Do you behave like this? Are you cemented firmly in your beliefs? Do you expound your beliefs as if they are facts? Do you tell the world what you believe? Do you try to make other people believe what you believe? Why?

People are personality dominated. Along with individual beliefs people are defined by how they behave and interact with the world. Due to this fact many behave in an aggressive all-knowing manner. With this personality as a basis, it causes them to attempt to make their beliefs heard no manner what the consequences.

Have you ever believed something, once-upon-a-time, but no longer believe it? When you did believe it, did your belief in it make you feel empowered? Did you try to make other people believe what you believe? What happened to that belief and why do you no longer believe it? Did you attempting to spread your belief to others alter the evolution of your life and/or did it alter the evolution and perhaps damage the life of someone else? If so, who is responsible and what are the consequences?

The thing about belief is, most people never look to the damage that their belief inflicts. They believe it, so it must be right. Right? They believe it, so others should believe it. Right?

Beliefs are large and they are small: large like religion and politics, small like personal opinions and ideas. But, large or small, beliefs have the potential to alter everything in your life-sphere, especially if you are one of those people who attempts to broadcast your beliefs to the world and try to make others believe what you believe.

What is a fact? A fact is an absolute, provable truth. What is a belief? Everything else.

What do you do with your beliefs and how do you do it? Your beliefs define your life. But, if you try to define the lives of others by your beliefs, you give birth to all of the problems of the world.

You should really be more than your beliefs. You should really care more about other people than what you believe in and why you believe it.

The Sage is silent. Thus, the Sage damages no-one and no-thing with his or her belief(s). The Sage leaves the world a better place. Do you?

*   *   *

05/07/16 17:28

When was the last time you said something nice about somebody?

Why did you say it?

When was the last time you said something bad about somebody?

Why did you say it?

*   *   *

05/07/16 17:28

Where do you live and how do your live?

What does where you live and how you live say about you?

The Price You Pay
05/07/16 08:04

       The fact of life is, there is always a price to pay. For anything that you do there is always the repercussion at the far side of the far side. All you have to do is look to the life of people who have done what you are doing and you can get a good idea of what that price will be. And, the louder, the more boisterous, the more interpersonally invasive what you do is, the larger the consequences are that you will pay.

       Every long-term martial artist I know; their hips, their knees, the ankles, their wrists, and/or their fingers are damaged or destroyed. Every musician has tinnitus, (ringing in the ears), and hearing loss. This same is true with gun enthusiasts, Harley Davidson riders, (motorcycles, especially customized ones, are loud). Smokers, forget about it. Have you ever watched a person die of lung cancer? It is bad. This, not to mention all the pollution they have unleased by throwing their cigarettes on the ground and polluting the air with their smoke. Drinkers kill how many people driving? And, destroy their own body. Gamblers lose it all and what do they end up with? Nothing. Druggies: lie, cheat, steal, and destroy every person's life they come into contact with. For what? All to get high. Even people who create art with paints and other toxic materials do a lot of damage to the environment and to their bodies. Yogis… Well, never mind, they don't do too much damage. ☺ But, the point is, anything that you choose to do, due to the fact that there is a rush value associated with it will more-than-likely mess up your life. There is no getting around it.

       This is true not only of what you do out there, but what you did in here — inside your mind. How you think makes you react to the world and to others in a specific manner. How much loss and destruction is associated with inter-personal demons like jealousy, judgment, rage, anger, and interpersonal denial? A lot. Do you embrace any of these thought-processes?

The formula for this cause/effect relationship to your life and the life of others is fairly obvious. You do something that alters the peace of the world or other people; anything that is loud, obtrusive, or invades the space of someone/anyone — if you do anything with a factual intention that invades the space of others not only damages the world but it comes back at you, making you pay for your sins.

So, how should you encounter life? The thing is, all of these, *"Things,"* are desire based activities. You were not born with the desire to do these things, you were not born with these personality traits, but it was YOU who decided to pursue them and embrace them. So, there is no one to blame but yourself when you encounter the repercussions of your actions and you WILL encounter the repercussions.

The fact is, most people don't care. They don't care because they are getting the rush that they get from doing what they do while they are doing it. They get the rush until the rush stops and they have to pay the cost. Then, it is all, *"Whoa is me."* But, you did it! You made a choice to do it! You did it and did not care about the effect it was having on you, your body, the people, and the world around you.

Here's the thing, if you can maintain conscious control over your life and not be lured into doing the things that we all know are damaging to our bodies, our mind, and the world around us, think how much better all-things in this world would be. …Think about you, have you been around someone who was doing something that really bothered you or something that really was damaging your life? You probably really hated it, didn't you? Do you ever think about the effect you are having on others when you do what you do? Do you ever think about the effect what you are doing is having on the world? If you don't, that means that you are a very selfish, thoughtless person. What happens to a selfish, thoughtless person? Sooner-or-later they pay the consequences for their actions.

What price are you willing to pay?

Who Do You Hate?
04/07/16 08:10

Are you one of those people who hates someone? Who is it? Is it someone you actually know like your ex-wife, ex-husband, ex-girlfriend, ex-boyfriend, boss, somebody who cheated you in a business deal, or someone who lied to you and messed up your life because of that lie? Or, is it someone you don't know: maybe a politician, a movie star, a musician, a sports personality, a news commentator, a reality TV star, an author, or a ??? But, why do you hate them?

If we look at life, there are those people who hate other people. In some cases, there is a very specific reason why a person hates someone. Perhaps that individual did something very specific to them that truly altered their life. In these incidences there is a cause and effect relationship. One person did one thing to one person and that person hates them because of it. Okay... I believe that if a person explains a logical reason for their feeling the way they do about a specific person, who did a specific thing to them, we can all understand the motivation for that emotion. But, the problem with harboring this type of negative emotion is that it is, in many cases, based upon perception. How many times has someone told you why they hated a person and you didn't get it — you thought that their emotion was based completely upon misplaced logic? But, what could you say or do? They feel the way they feel and that is that.

The thing is, we all do what we do in life. Many people do what they do with either very little forethought or none at all. They just run on desire and emotion and never take anyone or anything else into consideration. They just do what they do, want what they want. In some cases, they pass through much of their life while hurting no one, in other cases they create damage to every person they encountered. But, the question that has to be asked of the person who hates someone is, *"Was the damage created by the person you hate intentional and focused or was it simply a lapse of judgment."* No matter what the answer to that question the person feeling the hatred may come up with, it probably will not change their mind. But, it is essential to look at all sides of an issue before you ever decided to hate someone or choose to cast blame onto any person.

In other life cases, there is the person who hates someone that they do not even personally know for some ridiculously abstract reason. Maybe they play for a sports team that they don't like, maybe they are in a band and they hate their music, maybe they create art that they don't like, maybe they think that they are a bad actor, maybe they are simply jealous because the person they hate has found success in a field that they wish they were successful in. Or, maybe, they are simply not in-touch enough with their feelings to rationalize the truth about their misguided emotions and the only emotion they can come up with is that of hate.

Hate is a bad emotion. It causes people to do and say bad things. It causes a good percentage of the world's problems. But, hatred is almost universally born from the mind of one person. Though it may spread, the cause of hatred can be traced to one individual.

Let's look at you. Do you hate someone? Do you wish anyone ill-will? If so, why? Really, take a few moments, look at your life, study your thought patterns, and analyze if you hate someone and, if so, why do you hate them?

If there is someone you hate, what has that hatred caused you to do? What words have you spoken, what actions have you taken? Have any of those words or actions caused your hatred for that person to diminish?

The thing about hatred is that it is embraced by the individual who is not in conscious control of their emotions.

It is a random emotion that causes one to immediately feel adrenalized. From this, it can become an addictive emotion.

The person who feels hatred towards another person, particularly if it is someone that they do not personally know, is a person lost in a misguided sense of self. They do not know themselves, they are dissatisfied with their lives, or they would not be spending their time focusing on a person that they do not know and have never personally interacted with.

For the individual who hates a person for a specific reason, they do so to hold themselves locked into a precise place of time and space. They do not want to move on from that moment, so they hold onto their hatred. This may be because they are so locked into blaming the person for how they altered their life by doing what they did or it may be because they do not wish to let go and move onto a new and hopefully better life experience. Again, some people get locked into the adrenalizing rush of hatred. It is their drug of choice. So, they can't let go.

In life, we are all going to encounter people we do not like. In life, we are all going to have situations occur, brought about by specific people, that hurt us and changes our evolution forever. Though our desired evolution may have been changed by the actions of another person, that does not mean that we cannot become bigger, better, and more by learning from and overcoming whatever has been done to us.

Here's the thing… Think about the big picture. Are you doing something/anything with the intent to hurt someone? If you are, stop it! It's just wrong. You don't want a person's hatred to be focused your direction. Have you hurt someone, either intentionally or not? If you have, apologize. Saying, *"I'm sorry,"* goes a long way in life.

If you are on the other side of the spectrum — if you hate someone, particularly someone whom you have never personally interacted with; stop it! It just makes you look foolish and that you have accomplished nothing in your own right. And, if you are one of those people who associates with someone who hates somebody they have never met. Stop it! All they are doing is embracing negative energy which you are allowing to enter your life.

    If you have been hurt by someone and feel hatred towards them due to their action; has your hatred made you feel any better? Has it made your life any better? Probably not. So again, stop it! Stop allowing that person and what they did to you to hold control over your life.

    The best thing you can do to overcome anyone you hate is to work at becoming more than the person you hate. Achieve your own greatness. Do not allow anyone to maintain control over your emotions. Because if you do, if you hate anyone, that means that your mind is forever focused on them, instead of you. That means that you considered them more than you; which makes you less then them.

    Be more than hatred.

Repainting Your Canvas
03/07/16 14:35

For those of us who create art, especially the kind of art that is created upon a canvas, there is a certain tendency to want to keep what we have created forever. Be it bad or good, we don't want to destroy it because it depicts what we were creating when we were creating it.

For those of us who have sold our art, (well, at least for me), except for a few very specific pieces, I don't even remember what the what looked like... ...What I had done that went to the hands of others.

In a way that's good, I think. For then that art is free: free from my mind, free from my remembrance, and free from my rethinking it. In fact, there is only one piece that I gave away, one time a long time ago, that I wish I had kept. It was this very large oil painting of the Buddha. The person I gave it to and I went our separate ways long-long ago and I imagine she probably eventually threw it away — as it was really large. But, that is one of my stories, not yours, and I won't bore you with it here... So, most of the art I created that is out there is free... And, that is what art should be.

I know I've told this story somewhere before but about ten years ago I went though the enormous amount of paintings I had created on canvas and cut up a threw away a good percentage of them. Yes, it was based upon stuff I didn't like and/or didn't want to represent me in the long destiny of when... But, overall it was an enormously freeing process.

Today, I happened to looked through a few of my painting that were in a storage unit and the first one I saw I didn't like at all. It was actually only painted a few years ago but, damn, it had no semblance of developed style or substance what-so-ever. It was just paint on a canvas trying to present something I know not what.

I think back a number of years ago and this one friend was referencing this sax music I had created for a soundtrack way back in the way back when. I told him there's no way I could do that anymore. He joking expressed, *"You lost it..."* *"Yeah, I did,"* I answered. Looking at this painting today, I totally lost it... At least with that particular painting.

As I looked at it, my thought was, *"Should I paint over it?"* And, maybe I will...

Here's the thing, and this is the thing about life, while you are still here — still alive, you can repaint your canvas. You can change your life. Change what you are doing. And, change how you are doing it. When you're dead, you can't. Now, you can.

I think most people don't do this though. They don't even think about it. They get into the pattern of their life and they never even think about changing what they are doing, how they are living their life, or anything else. They just do what they do the way they do it and that is that. But, you can change! You can become something different! You can become something better!

On the spiritual path, particularly on the Eastern spiritual path, your guru gives you a new name once you have been initiated. This is done in order to separate you from who you used to be and allow you to become someone new. I know, I used the new name(s) I was given. But, the problem is, we here in the West we are in the West. We have our names, our social security numbers, our everything pretty much etched into stone. Plus, it is very hard to go and tell the masses, who do not abide by, condone, or understand the Eastern metaphysical tradition at all. Thus, they don't want to call you some weird Sanskrit name. So, changing is very hard. But, it can be done.

Now, you don't have to change your name if you don't want to. But, you can change your life. You can choose to repaint your canvas, stop associating with those who do

not lead you to your higher-self, and actually become a better version of you.
    You should try it.

Reaching Out with Kindness
02/07/16 08:46

How do you encounter life? Do you meet it head-on, face-to-face with selfish thoughts, aggressive actions, and behavior demeaning to others? Or, do you smile, reach out a helping hand, and forgive instead of unleashing harsh condemnation?

How you choose to encounter life is how your life will be interpreted by others and will lead to the type of life-interactions you will have throughout your existence. And yes, how you live your life is your choice.

When you have been sad, angry, hurt, lied to, cheated, or beaten down by life who do you think about when you remember those incidences? First of all, you remember the person who brought those situations into your life. And, you most likely remember them in a negative light. Second, you remember the person who reached out a hand of helpfulness and kindness to you. That person will forever hold a place in your heart as they were the one who came to you and only expressed loving, helpful kindness.

From this simply case of life-remembrance you should easily see the best way to behave in life. But, many people do not take the time to chart their life. They do not take the time to set about on a conscious course of life-affirming action(s). Instead they are simply controlled by negative emotions instead of consciously deciding which emotions that they actually will embrace.

Do you ever ask yourself why you are doing what you are doing before you are doing it? Or, do you just do it?

Do you ever ask yourself why you are doing what you are doing before you are doing it? If you preform this conscious mental action, do you actually come up with a precise conclusion based upon a desired end-result? And, what is your desired end-result? Are you hoping to help someone or something? Are you trying to help yourself? Or, are you attempting to hurt someone or something? Or, are you just doing it to do it because you can?

Let's look at this situation for a moment... If you are trying to help yourself that can be understood to be a fairly common human desire. But, does your helping yourself hurt anyone else in the process. If you helping yourself hurts anyone, then no matter what your motivation, it cannot be seen as a conscious, good, or kind action.

If you are actually attempting to hurt anyone, for any reason at any level, who and what does that make you? What gives you the right? And, what do you think the end-results of your life is going to equal if you have unleashed this type of lower-self motivated behavior and activity onto the world?

People become empowered in various ways throughout their existence. They find a method to express themselves. Some find that they can encounter some sort of self-worth by embracing and exhibiting negative behavior. But, what is the result of negative behavior? Have you ever actually studied its patterns? Negative people think negative thoughts and continually encounter negative life experiences. It is as simple as that.

The opposite is also true, however. Think about the person who reaches out their hand to help people. They are always thought of as nice, kind, and giving. They forever meet people who want to thank them for their positive actions. And, just as we discussed in the beginning of this essay, who do you remember and how do you remember them? You remember the person that hurt you and you remember the person that helped you. One you think of negatively, the other you think of with loving positivity.

How do you want your life to be remembered? How do you want people to think about you?

My advice, do positive things, do good things, turn off your ego and help people whenever you can. Never pass judgment. Ask forgiveness for any wrongs you have committed and erase their trail of transmittal into the future.

This is your life. This life is your choice. How you live it will effect your forever and may lead to affecting the forever of other people. Thus, only say and do good things. Only help and never hurt. Only care and not judge. Mostly, be kind.

* * *

01/07/16 13:40

If you have created nothing, you have nothing that anyone can criticize.

* * *

30/06/16 14:11

Just because you demand something doesn't mean that you deserve to receive it.

Take and Make:
Making Money Off the Labor of Others
30/06/16 09:13

The United States of America has had a rich history of making money off of the labor of others. Well, hell... That has been the case with the whole world. Whether it was the slave trade, the master and servant relationships of bosses to their employees, or the people who simply figure out a way around the system and con people into getting them to work for free while they soak up the money, this has been, is, and probably always will be the case.

Have you, personally, ever worked for someone, getting paid a very low wage, while you watched the people at the top living the life of embellishment? It is a very eye-opening experience. You need to live, you need a way to live, so you have to do what you have to do to be able to live. You do your job for a reason. Yet, you have to observe those at the top of the food chain living large off of your actions. In some ways this is a good life experience because it really teaches a person the true realities of existence.

Many people find a way to dance their way through life, living off of their parents, family money, or whatever, and they never truly come to learn the inner-realities of making a living. That is to say, they never truly learn the realities of the absolute need to make a living or die.

If we all open our eyes and ears, we can hear about the horrors that are currently taking place in Africa and the Middle-East. Though geographic locations may change, these horrors have been going on forever. There are the people who are just trying to survive and then there are those who have found themselves in a position of power or authority using the lives of these people.

But, do you watch, do you listen, do you care? Or, do you only think about yourself?

Which position are you in? Are you on the lower-level of the relationship struggling to survive or are you the one in a position of authority; taking?

In the modern era many people have found a way to take and make via the internet. I've been an outspoken opponent of this forever, as the banner says, *"Internet piracy is not a victimless crime."* It is not. People get hurt. But, do these people who take and make via the internet care? No. Or, they wouldn't do it.

In every industry I have ever been involved in, I have observed those who lived well off of the labor of others. Whether it was the music industry, the film industry, or the martial arts, there are those who find their way to the top and then pay those below them either nothing or close to nothing, while they live large. But, everyone has a reason, everyone has a justification for doing what they do…

The fact is, if you take anything from anyone for any reason, you are stealing. Not only are you stealing from the person you are taking from but you are creating a situation where others believe that it is okay to steal. Think about this, is it?

You may justify in your mind that what you are doing is allowing you to survive in a manner that you deem appropriate. But, if you don't care about the cost to the lives of others that means that you don't care about the cost to the lives of others. Are you any better than the people in African and the Middle East that are destroying the lives of people simply as a means to fulfill their desires?

Each person sets a course for their life. Each person must find a way to survive. Religion promises hell to those who do bad things to people. That would be great if it were fact. But, none of us know whether it is or is not. So, all we are left with is ourselves and the choices we choose to make. It is us who must decide to do the right thing. …To do the thing that provides for the betterment of the all and does not steal from, damage, or injure the life of any person in the process of our finding a means of survival.

Who are you? What are you doing and why? What is your justification? Is your justification hurting anyone in the process of doing what you are doing? If you were asked for an answer, what would you say to god?

Two Sides of the Same Street
29/06/16 12:36

As the hit song from the 80s ideally describes, *"Nobody walks in L.A."* That is so true, you rarely see adults walking any distance of anywhere in L.A.

That being said, today, I was driving down the street and I noticed two people walking virtually perpendicular to one another. One was this beautiful Asian woman who had insanely long hair. By the clothing she wore you could tell she was affluent. One the other side of the street was this aging white guy. You could see he was homeless as he was carrying all these dirty bags full of his stuff. There they were, in totally different places in life, but they were walking right across the street from one another.

This sight was an exceedingly good depiction of life. There are the haves and the have-nots. Some of this is based upon birth and whom you were born to. But, in other cases, it is simply defined by the choices you make. You make that one bad choice, you do that one wrong thing, you make that one wrong turn, and your life ends up destroyed.

We are all dominated by outside influences. We are all dominated by the people we come to know and come to associate with. We are all dominated by the types of jobs we can find. We are all dominated by physiological determinates. We are all dominated by our class and where we find ourselves in culture and in history. All of these things form the person we are to become. And, many of them can be blamed for the choices we make. Many, but not all.

The fact is, your life is largely defined by what you decided to do with each set of circumstance you are handed. It is you who must make the choice will you do the legal, right thing or will you partake of something on the dark side. Your life. Your choice. But, the implications of that choice can be all-encompassing.

Have you ever known someone who did something wrong and ended up in jail? When they got out, was their life ever the same? Probably not. Have you ever known someone who got lost in drink or drugs? How did that affect their life? Could they stop and if they did stop was their life ever the same? Have you ever known someone who believed in an investment and sank all of their money into it? What happened to them when their investment didn't pay off and they were left penniless? The list goes on but it all equals one thing, you make a choice in life and sooner-or-later that choice is going to own you.

What you choose to do, even if you come from a loving, affluent family, has the potential to change your everything.

There is a fine line between success and failure in life. You do one wrong thing and…

This being said, it is essential that you live your life very consciously and do what you do very consciously. Doing bad things, saying bad things, associating with bad people, and making bad choices have one end result, your life will end up bad.

What side of the street do you want to walk on?

*   *   *
                              29/06/16 12:35

How is life working out for you?

* * *

29/06/16 12:34

If you are unhappy, you will find something to make you unhappy.

If you are angry, you will find something to make you angry.

If you are depressed, you will find something to make you depressed.

If you are happy, you will find something to make you happy.

* * *

29/06/16 12:34

What have you done?

How do you want your life to be remembered?
29/06/16 08:57

Throughout my life I've watched as people continually shift the focus from themselves and what they are or are not accomplishing to placing the spotlight on others. Whether it has been in the world of rock n' roll where people would argue about who was the better guitar player, to the world of filmmaking where actors and filmmakers would criticize other actors and filmmakers, onto the marital arts where insecurity reigns supreme and low-level martial artists are constantly finding new reasons to criticize other martial artists. But, why do people do this? Why do people wish to find fault in others? In a nutshell the answer is, a person wants to find fault in someone else so that they can look like the authority on the subject — so that they can appear as if they are better and/or more. But, are they? What have they personally accomplished? And, if they are focusing on someone else that already proves that the person they are discussing has accomplished more than them because that is where their focused is being placed.

Okay… But, what does all this prove? What does one person criticizing and critiquing another person prove? It proves nothing.

Life is about what you personally create. Your life is about what you personally do. What you think and what you say about another person, be it bad or good, is irrelevant to the greater course of your life as any other person, and what you think about them, has nothing to do with who or what you create or become. For this reason, all energy spent focusing on someone else only diminishes who you are in the eyes of the world and/or what you can ultimately become, as your time has been wasted not focusing on the essential element of your life, you. You have instead spent it focusing on someone else.

Some people spend their life helping others. This is a very good thing. But, do people who live this life of service spend their time criticizing others who are also givers, stating that they are not doing enough or that what they are doing is in some manner wrong? No. They give and help and they allow others to give and help. These people are the ideal example of the way one should walk through life. Yes, they may know about the existence of other helpers but they do not waste their time criticizing them. They simply continue to do what they have chosen to do and that is to help the world in whatever way that they can.

At each juncture of your life you truly need to take a long hard look at yourself and what you are doing and why. This is perhaps one of the biggest flaws of humanity, they do not look at themselves. Instead, they find it much easier to focus on something or someone outside of themselves.

The fact is, criticism is easy. It takes no effort. All you have to do is criticize. But, what does that equal? It equals nothing. You have not done anything, you have not accomplished anything. All you have done is place further focus on the person you are criticizing.

Do you want to be remember in life? Do you want to do something good? Do you want to be seen as a contributor to the great whole? If you do, then there is only one way to do that and it is not by critiquing someone who actually has accomplished something, it is is by actually doing something good in your own right. For this is the only way that true life-accomplishment is actualized. This is the only way to been seen as a true contributor. This is the only way to be viewed as some-one who did some-thing other than simply a person who talks about other people.

Who are you? How do you want your life to be remembered?

*   *   *

29/06/16 08:21

If you are thinking about someone else that means that the focus of your life is on something that you have no control over.

Rudraksha: The Most Holy Beads of Shiva
29/06/16 07:30

I was in a shop today. I walked up to the cash register to pay for my items and I noticed two very interesting women. One was the cashier. She was African-American, had her head clean-shaven on one side but had very long straight hair covering the rest of her head. She had one of those very unique faces. The kind you study, wondering why is she so interesting? The other girl, the customer, was a very tall girl, maybe six-foot, three. She has platinum blonde dreadlocks and spoke with a slight European accent; probably German.

The cashier inquired about the necklace the customer was wearing. *"These are rudraksha prayer beads. These are the most holy beads of Shiva."* The cashier didn't know who Shiva was and asked if it was a place. *"Oh no, it is the god I worship,"* explained the girl. *"You should really look into him."* Okay...

Anyway, the girl turned slightly and I saw the beads. They weren't rudraksha, they were actually sandalwood. No big deal, really... But, it just goes to the source of life and people's beliefs.

Somehow, somewhere, someway, someone told this girl that what she had was a rudraksha mala, (prayer beads). But, they weren't. It's anybody's guess why she thought this and, I suppose, in the greater scheme of life, it really doesn't matter. It only matters to the true Shaivite, (a worshiper of the Hindu god, Shiva).

But, this is the thing I have always discussed about people penetrating other world cultures. No matter how much you want to be a part of it, you are not. There are subtitles that every person from India (for example) would know; i.e. what type of prayer beads a person is wearing. Outside of that, there are knowledgeable people but these people are not born of that culture and will never truly understand the subtitles — though they may play the game of dress up: i.e. have dreadlocks, wear prayer beads, and tell people they worship Shiva. But, go to India and it is a whole new ballgame. Even me, who lived there, was initiated there, and has spent a lot of time there — I understand that there is an essence of that culture and that religion that I will never truly know. Even though I do know what is and/or is not a rudraksha mala.

Now, I am not saying, do not expand you mind. I am also not saying, if you are drawn to a distant religion, do not study and practice it. What I am saying is that you must keep the game of, *"Dress up,"* in check. You most forever forgo the outward symbolism and the evangelism because the fact is, you may be getting it wrong.

For whatever karamic reason we are born into the culture we are born into. We may love it, we may hate it, but IT is who and what we are. It is the culture that shaped us. Thus, we will never be free from that culture. We are part and parcel of that culture. We can go anywhere on this globe that we can go. We can study every text on any subject that we choose to believe in. We can earn a degree in the subject, we can be initiated into the religion, but the essence of who we are is not THAT. THAT will forever be something outside of ourselves. We are who we are on the inside, created by our culture. We may have a million desires to be something else but, in essence and in fact, that is not who we truly are.

Just like many of the inhabitants of India would love to come to America, many a Westerner has looked to the East. Me too. But, through trial and experience I know, at the end of the day, who and what I am. I do not try to be anything else. I do not play dress up. (At least not anymore). ☺

So do what you do. But, remember who you are. No matter how hard you try to run from it, at the end of the day, that is all you can truly be.

* * *

29/06/16 07:24

What thoughts fill your mind?

* * *

29/06/16 07:24

Nobody cares what you think.

Good is Good, Bad is Bad, and You Know the Difference
28/06/16 08:27

There is forever the quest for the good in life. To become better, know more, and do things that the world will find appealing. That is to say, most people want to do good things.

There is a subset of humanity, however, who are on a quest to embrace the negative. They are always critical, criticizing, down on someone, something (everything). They say negative words. They always have something negative to say about someone whenever another person is brought up. They are attracted to those of like-mind — those who focus on the critical and the negative — those who insult, berate, and demonize others.

When you are saying something positive, you know what you are saying. You know what you are saying is going to make people feel better. You know that even if someone is down, by saying something positive to them you may be providing the key to make them feel better. The energy of the words you are speaking and the caring actions you are taking are going to have a positive effect on all those they encounter.

When you are saying something negative, you know that you are saying; something negative. You know what the source is, you. You know what the outcome will be, negativity. So, why do you do it? What is your motivation for saying something negative about someone, anyone, or anything? Do you even know?

This is perhaps the biggest problem in life and why so much negativity has been unleashed to the world. People do what they do because they are lost in a negative sense of self and are lashing out to the world. They are angry and they want to hurt other people so they too will be angry and so that the world will understand and embrace their individualized negativity.

The person who behaves in this manner is not whole. But, why? Why can't you say to them, *"What you are saying is bad. Stop it!"* But, they will not. The reason is, through time they have come to be engulfed in this mindset of negativity. They are lost in their negative self.

Most people who exist on this plane of consciousness do not even take the time to question their own actions. They understand what they are doing and saying is negative and that it will hopefully hurt someone but they cannot step outside of themselves long enough to care.

Perhaps this is the true measure of humanity, someone who cares. Perhaps this is also the true measure of the bad person, someone who does not.

The fact is, many people hide their self-embellishing negativity. Some claim spirituality on the outside but are a demon on the inside. The rich create or give to charities to make themselves look philanthropic. All this, while they line their own bank accounts.

What it comes down to is, what do you think, what do you say, what do you do? For these actions, based upon the most elemental level of human existence, are the birthplace for all you will encounter in life.

For example, did you ever know one of those people who embraces the negative? Maybe you are one of these people. Have you watched their life over time? Did it ever get any better? Were they ever more loved through time? Did their life-philosophy ever come to be universally embraced? Did they ever become more respected or accomplished? Or, did they simply wallow in their negative mindset, never evolving to anything more over time?

In all life equations, the person is the key to the answer. How they behave, equals who they become. Some people do evolve, change their negative ways, and become more. Many do not. But, the simple way to see where a life defined by negativity will lead is to look at the person who is or has been defined by negativity. Who are they? What are they? Where are they? Have they accomplished? Are they loved? Or, are they only embraced by others who wish to dwell in their realms of negativity?

If you say something negative, you know what you are doing. If you are taking a negative action, you know what you are doing. If you say something positive, you know what you are doing. If you take a positive action, you know what you are doing.

If you seek out negativity, judgment, criticism, hatred; all of these things will embellish your life. If you allow yourself to be lured in by someone who embraces these things, their negativity will come to define who you are and what you become. Just as if you always look for the positive, always try to do the positive, the positive will become your definition. Which one do you think is better?

Catch yourself. Don't say negative things, they are negative. Don't find a reason or a justification to do negative things, they are negative. Instead, no matter what you are thinking or feeling, force yourself to embrace the positive. From this, positivity will overtake your life and all will appreciate what you give to the world.

When There is No Logical Explanation
28/06/16 07:33

I always find the peculiarities of life very interesting. …The things in life that you can find no logical explanation for.

For example, today I went to get into my car and I noticed that there was a rock sitting on my seat. Now, this was no small pebble like the kind that maybe would get stuck in the sole of your shoe. This was a fairly good sized rock. I picked it up, studied it, and then throw it away. But, how did it get there? My car doors were locked. I was nowhere recently where that style of rock may have been found. So, I don't know? Yet, it was there.

Has anything like that ever happened to you? Though not too frequently, I imagine that it has. It has pretty much happened to everyone that I know.

I think back a number of years when something like this happened before. I went out and when I came home a few hours later three of my interior doors had been closed. I checked everything to make sure no one had broken in or anything like that. But nothing, everything was fine. The only reason this truly concerned me was that my cats had been cut off from their food and water. But, since it was only for a couple of hours, they were fine. But still, how and why did this happen? There was no logical explanation. I guess just some aberrant wind from a couple of different directions had blown in and closed the doors.

When these thing happen to you, how do you behave? Does it make you paranoid, wondering who did what and why? Or maybe, you just chalk it up the antics of mystical spirits or gnomes. Whatever the case, it does make you question. At least it makes me question — wonder why about the question of why. Why did this happen and why did it happened to me.

Other times in my life things have occurred that were strange but they had logic attached to them. One time I had no gas left in my tank at all. I pulled into a gas station to fill up but I found no credit cards or driver's license in my wallet. I thought back to the day before and I realized that someone must have broken into my locker at the gym, because that was the only time I was separated from my wallet. They must have had some way to pop my lock, get my credit cards, and then relock the lock, leaving me none the wiser.

So, there I stood at the pump. I was actually pretty screwed because I only a couple of dollars in my pocket and with no credit card or ATM I had no way to buy much gas. But, I was able to purchase just enough to get me home.

Sadly though, I really like that driver's license picture. You know how most of them are not very good. But, that one I actually liked… But, it was gone forever…

As for the the thieves, they were focused on what they were after. They took my credit cards and driver's license but they didn't check my pockets. They left a Rolex in my side pocket. Good for me, bad for them. Because that was one of my favorite watches. I never took anything into the gym again!

As for life, weird stuff just happens sometimes. Some things can be traced back and an explanation can be found. I mean there's cameras everywhere now; someone knows everything. But, other stuff, you will never know how, when, where, or why. It just is… Left only to the imagination about what actually caused it.

Kind of makes life interesting, don't you think?

* * * 27/06/16 13:07

Someone tells you something.

It turns out to be a lie.

What happened if you believed them?

*   *   *

27/06/16 13:05

The world is full of conspiracy theorists. They find all kinds of supposed facts to support their claims. But, facts are not facts unless they are facts. Most facts are simply one person's perception of the way they want things to be.

The Demands of Others
27/06/16 08:55

Each of us has people in our life whom we know and interact with on a frequent basis. These people are a part of our life so we see them all of the time. We know them, we understand who they are, and we know how they are going to act and behave. We know them, so we know this.

How are you expected to behave? Do certain people in your life expect you to behave in a particular manner? And, because they expect you to behave in a particular manner, do you behave in that way?

Life is based upon human interaction. Much of our fun, happiness, and, in fact, sadness is based upon our human interactions. We chart a pathway through life defined by what we do and whom we do it with.

How do you do it? Do you do it the way other people expect you to do it? Or, do you do it with a devil-may-care attitude; acting and doing only as you please. If you follow this path, then you are most likely more alone than you are interactive, as everyone wants to interact with an individual who behaves in a way that is predictable and palatable.

Who are you within your life? Who do you spend the most amount of time with? Do you spend much of your time alone? Do people like you? Do people dislike you? Are you kind, caring, and helpful or are you negative, judgmental, and mean? Is your life prone to calm, happy interpersonal interactions or is your life defined by outbursts, childish tantrums, spouting judgments, and/or physical or verbal violence?

You are the source of whom you interact with in life. You, and how you behave, defines who will be willing to interact with you. Thus, you create the possibilities in your world from how you choose to behave — defined by the expectations of those around you.

In life, some people demand that you behave in a certain way. But, who are they to demand anything? Certainly, in our childhoods we are forced to behave in a particular manner defined by the rules of our parents and/or school authorities. Many of us run into problems due to our rebellion against these rules and regulations. But, that is a natural process; us finding out who we are defined within the parameters of society.

As we move into adulthood, however, there are those who attempt to define how we behave by what they believe to be the proper format of behavior. They want from us what they want from us. They want us to act in the manner that they deem appropriate. They want us to be the person they want us to be.

Of course, all attempts at manipulation are based upon insecurity. And, as we all know, insecurity is developed in the person who has no true sense of self or accomplishment. As certain people's lives are defined by insecurity, they then try to take control over anything that they can; be that the weaker minded, the insecure, those with an addictive personality, the young, and/or those who seek out negativity as a sourcepoint for their life. Whatever the case, these people, due to their lack of accomplishment and self-worth, attempt to spread their misguided domination by attempted control over the lives of other people's human behavior.

In some cases, people allow this type of person to actually control their behavior. They do this for any number of reason: love, family, a desire to be accepted, the need to be seen as part of something, and even, in the more obvious cases, to keep a job. But, within all of this there is an inner-person insides all of us who is who we truly are. Though some of us have lost that person due to allowing others to control us.

Who is inside of you? Who and what are you when the controlling hands of the outside world have been lifted?

Are you actually the person who you present to the world? Or, are you someone else who has been lost due to acting the way other people have expected you to act?

We can all say, it is best to be who you truly are and act the way you wish to act. This is especially the case for those with an enlightened mindset who actually try to become the best person they can be. Not all of us are like that, however. Some people are lost in the negative refection of themselves and no matter what you say to them they are not, (and never will be), whole enough to take the steps to make themselves better. They are more willing to remain lost in their lower, judgmental self, than to open their mind and embrace the greater good.

With this as a basis of understanding, all any of us can do is be the person we are and follow the pathway to an elevated mind. We must understand that each person is who they are and allow them to be who and what they truly are — never attempting to take control over anyone and not allowing anyone to take control over us — particular those who focus their lives upon the negative or domineering style of behavior.

As long as who you are is good, be who you are. As long as who you are is hurting no one, be the best YOU that you can be. Consciously remove the factors of domination from your life that keep you from being who you truly are and become the best presentation of yourself.

* * *

27/06/16 07:33

If you have demons inside of you then you look for demons everywhere you go and in everyone you meet.

There's Millions of People Who Are Suffering
26/06/16 07:39

Have you even gotten into the shower and the water was too cold? Have you ever taken a shower and the water was too hot? Though you take a shower in the same place everyday, for some reason, on this day, you just have a very hard time getting the water just right.

I think back to one of the times I was in Burma. I was twenty-five and I was staying at the only hotel that was in existence, at the time, in Mandalay. I had woken up one morning and I went to hit the shower before I went out to the day. The water pressure was *ify,* the temperature of the water was inconsistent, the floor of the shower was a cold cement basin, and it was all making me really frustrated. Anyway, finishing my shower, having my breakfast in the hotel restaurant, I went out and was walking around the streets. As I was, I saw several of the locals taking their morning shower/bath. They were in front or to the side of their small wooden homes. What they had was a bucket full of water that they would dip their washcloth or a sponge into and wash themselves down with it. One guy, when he was done, took the bucket and poured it over his head. That was his shower. I wondered how the he liked the temperature and/or the water pressure?

Here's the point, there are so many people out there who do not have any of the comforts that we do. Yet, we are the one's complaining. We are the one's obsessing about some thing, some object that we desire, or some person. We are doing all we can for what WE want but we are nothing for anyone else. We are not thinking about anyone else but ourselves.

What do you do to help the people who are suffering? What do you do to help the people, across the globe, that actually need help? Do you spend you time mentally masturbating on the internet or do you get off of your ass and go out and do something that actual help someone who needs help?

If you do not take your mental focus off of yourself and what you want to do when you want to do it, your life is meaningless. If you do not get out there and do something positive, and actually helpful, to make the lives of those in-need better, your life is meaningless. If you focus your energy on hurting anyone, no matter what your motivation, instead of helping someone/everyone, your life is meaningless.

People are in need all around us. You don't have to go to Burma to find them. There are millions of people who are suffering, are you one of them? Probably not. If you are not, then get out there and help someone. Get out of your own head and do something good. For this is the only true measure of a person. This is the only thing that you can actually take pride in accomplishing. This is the only thing that all humanity will actually applaud. The only thing that truly matters in life is, who are you helping, who's life are you making better, and who's life have you removed pain from?

Today's a good day to start. Get off your butt and go out and do something that actually helps someone.

Why Don't You Paint?
25/06/16 03:27

There is this one statement that you always here whenever you are in a museum or gallery where they are exhibiting abstract art, *"Anybody can do that."* I certainly have heard that about my art. It always makes me smile.

I was thinking back to when I used to live at this one place in Hermosa Beach. I had a really big kitchen and I would staple my large canvases to the wall when I painted. I would paint late into most every night. When I would go out of the country, and I was traveling all of the time back then, I would give my one friend the keys to my place so he could come over and get my mail and stuff. One day he was over, just before I was to leave, and he went into this long discourse about my art, abstract art in general, *"Your stuff is crap,"* the, *"Anybody can do that,"* thing, and why bother in the first place? I could have taken offense. But, I get it... A lot of people think that way. They see the world the way the world is expected to be seen and they don't waste their time or their money on anything else. And, believe me, if you paint you understand: paint and canvas and brushes and stuff can be very expensive.

Now, I've written a lot about art over the years. Certainly, not as profoundly as say Kandinsky and others. But, I get it... Art is art only truly in the mind of the artist. And, whether your art is painting, photography, jewelry making, filmmaking, or whatever, you may not find a large audience for what you're doing, especially if what you are doing is somewhere outside of the norm and you don't have a big gallery owner or publicist marketing your stuff to the world.

The fact is, people like to judge. And, the judgment of art is one of the easiest things anyone can do, even if they love art... They can simply hate an artist or an art piece and that is okay — no further explanation necessary.

But, on a more philosophical level, I think most people really need to shake their life up. They need to do this as most, go through life so contrived, so predictable. They never take a step into the world of the abstract. They never try to embrace something new and totally different. They never try to paint.

I think most people, if they pick up a brush try to make something, they expect to paint like the old-school masters. They want to do that kind of art, if they do art at all. But, that is expecting the near-impossible unless you go through years of training. But, what you can do is do the art of feeling. You can make color swirl — you can make nothing at all.

The fact is, even this style of art takes a little practice. Just like Zen, embracing the nothing takes a little time. But, life is so full of the, "All that is." It is so full of it that it is already there. So, taking a moment to do the nothing allows you to embrace a moment of unexpected excellence. It allows you to BE without try to be.

Now, to the critic, the traditionalist, or to the uptight individual, who's mind is already made up, they will have a million reasons not to try. If they did try, they would probably try to fail, so that they would not have to do it again. But, try this, remove your mind and your judgments from the equation — even if only for a moment. Take a brush, get some paper or a canvas, grab some paint and, like a child, simply express nothing with no intentions upon your page. I mean, really… Try it. It truly will give you a moment of meditative freedom and you may really find a new space of peaceful, passive expression that will give you an outlet for the artist in you that you never believed was there.

Yeah, maybe everyone can do it. But, everyone doesn't do it. Try it. You never know how it may change your life.

Patterns of Diction
24/06/16 14:38

    Kind of picking up from my previous blog… I was over at my friend's studio a little while back. He's a consummate jokester like me. We laugh all the time we're together. Whenever he finds something about me on the internet, either positive or negative, he shows me and turns it into a joke. We laugh and laugh. I do the same for him.

    The other day he showed me this site where this one guy was raising questions about my background trying to cast shade on me. As I read what was written, it was all so familiar. It took me a few minutes and then I realized it was written by this one guy who used to post on the martial art discussion boards back in the earlier days of the internet. Though he was using a different/false name for this posting, it was definitely him. He really gave himself away when he used this one term that I had never seen used by any other martial artist but him. I laughed and laughed. I wanted to call him out and post to the posting who he really was. But, I realized, he would just do what everyone else does on the internet: lie and deny. But, it is him.

    Here's the thing, we all have a way of writing. Me, I tend to be wordy and punctuate heavily. I grew to this style of writing due to all the studies I have written for academic journals. A couple of the martial art editors I have written for have really given me grief about this. They say that the average martial artist only has a high school education and you have to write for the 8th grade reader. I never believed that. So, though I try to be simple in my sentence construction for the martial art's editors, I write what I write and they can edit me as need be.

    Anyway, it was so obvious it was this guy. I'm told he also posted to another website, using a different screen name but the diction was the same. I guess he really went off on me on that site and it must have been too trollish so they took it down. It's like this guy is locked in some twenty-year deep time warp. He was writing the same stuff about me way back when. Get over it! Get a life! What is missing in your own life that you are even thinking about me? I mean, if those aforementioned martial art sites were still up I could probably find the same statements he is writing about me now, written about me from twenty years deep.

Now, I've told this story before, but, way back in the way back when, I remember the first time this happened to me. There was this martial artists/university employed Ph.D. who wrote this whole piece, complete with footnote, totally bashing me. I read it and laughed and laughed. As I said then, *"It was so National Enquirer."* Now, I guess I would say, "It was so TMZ."

The thing about it was, the guy wrote the piece about me, but I was alive. Yet, he didn't contact me. He didn't ask me anything about what he was saying. Thus, he didn't check his facts. He just wrote it as if it was some scholastic paper. But, for any academic paper, don't you go to the source if they are still alive? He didn't. He just wanted to make me look bad. When some of the people who, *"Liked me,"* attempted to post rebuttals to the website, the webmaster disavowed them. So much for fairness.

I actually wrote a piece about this experience titled, *"Enlightenment is Easy. It's Life That's Hard."* It was on this website for a long time, now it is in one of my books.

The fact is, had that guy reached out to me and taken the time to get to know me, maybe we could have been friends. He didn't. He just wanted to slam me. Same with the guy that I write this blog about. But, when all you do is focus on criticism then all you are left with is anger and negativity. This is a choice that some people make. Me, I prefer conversation compared to argument; trust as opposed to accusation.

Anyway… I laughed then as I do now.

Here's the thing about me... Let's clear it up right now for anyone out there wondering or for those of you lost in some twenty-year deep time warp... I don't care about accolades! I don't care about titles or degrees! Yes, I've worked hard and earned the one's I've received. But, they do not define me! I disavow them. Like I always say, *"If you're claiming to be a Master, that probably means that you are not!"* I claim nothing! The only reason I have anything listed on the bio or FAQ page of my website is so that people won't have to ask. ...So, the person who is curious can know a little about my background and possibly understand why I do what I do. This is also the reason I do not post to other websites. Like I have long said, *"You can only play in your own playground."* Other people, who like what I do or even those who hate me for some undisclosed, undefined reason can post stuff out there but not me. I don't play that game and this is why I so rarely know what's out there about me unless someone, like my friend, brings it to my attention.

I do what I do in life. More people like what I do than don't, that's how and why I can keep doing it. I live my life for rising human consciousness, positive self-awareness, and for the art I create. That's it! That's all I do! I live a simple life. So, don't try to define me by whatever self-concocted, judgmental values you possess. Don't try to define me by what you are looking for, because that's not me! Worry about yourself and your own life, not mine.

Wow, that sounds pretty intense. It makes me smile...

But, more to the point, there are all of these people out there who are going to try to define you by how they judge reality. Maybe they are envious of you. Maybe they are angry at you for some nondescript, illogical reason. Maybe they just want to cause your life grief because they have nothing better to do than waste their time on the internet trying to cast shade where there is none. All you can do is live your life and not let them suck you into their melodrama.

Be who you are/what you are. Create your life as best as you can create your life. Because really, that's all any of us can do... And, to people like the one I am discussing who cast their judgements to the internet, they will never be happy with any answer you give them anyway... They will find some fault in it: someway, somehow. So, don't waste your time attempting to appease them.

Now, I will need to shift the topic(s) of this blog back to the more artsy, human consciousness sort of nonsense. Rock on! ☺

Don't Suck Me Into Your Melodrama
24/06/16 14:37

Throughout time there have been people who have achieved great success. In times gone past, the more successful a person was the more they became sheltered from the common man and the world in general. By whatever means, those with success became more-and-more protected. Times have changed... The flood gates have opened and now those with success allow the entire world into their life. They do this predominately by participating in social media. They tell the world where they are, what they are doing, who they are doing it with, what they love, what they hate, and how they are feeling in any given moment. Some, see this as an obligation. But, is it?

If we look to the common person, who is yet to achieve, why do they participate in social media? Most, do it to find those of like mind which will possibly result in friendships and/or interpersonal relationships. Then, there are some who are driven; those who want to get their thoughts and beliefs out the world — they want their opinion(s) to be known so they take it to social media to tell the world, *"How it is."* Their opinion must be right, right? Well, at least they think so... Me, I have always found that type of person annoying. They are the know-it-all and they generally base all that they know upon condemnation and negativity. When they place it in social media they release this negativity to the world. I believe that is not a good thing to do.

But, back to the point, many of those who have actually achieved success, open up their life and their mind to the world via social media — letting all those who want to enter, come in. From this, there has been born all kind of crimes, threats, accusations, and deluded self-orientated actions taken by the mentally unstable masses, and there are lot of them out there. These actions have hurt a lot of people.

We've all seen it in the news. But, who's fault is it? By opening up a line of dialog via social media, many who possess an altered frame of understanding then believe that they actually have a right to enter a person's life. Someone had opened the door. And, though they most certainly never expected the consequences, they were the one who began to play the game. So, again, who's fault is it?

If we look to times gone past, there were those who were successful. Then, there was those who were not. The person who was not, never had the chance to interact with those who were. That is, not unless, they worked very-very hard and rose up through the ranks and achieved something great on their own. Then, they moved up in class.

Today, everybody believes that they have already achieved. Anybody can say anything. They can interact with anybody. From this, all those with success have done, (and, in fact, anyone who climbs on the social media bandwagon), is allowing anyone, no matter what their intentions, into the inner realms of their life.

Commonality of a time and a space in history is the commonality of a time and space in history. Social media is the commonality of this period. Think back to when you were young, in a time gone past, there was probably a band or a musician or an actor that you really liked but you had no way, other than via magazines or the news, to know anything about them. Today, you can know, or at least believe that you know, everything about them: what they are doing and what they are thinking. This is good and this also is bad for all the illusion of distance has been removed — all of the need to actually become successful, in your own right, in order to interact with these people, has been removed.

The fact is, you may think that you know everything about a person. But, you do not. You can never truly know what is in another person's mind or in their heart if you do not personally know them. And, this is where all the nightmares of social media begin. You (they) have allowed people to have an open door into your life. You have given them access. Thus, they believe they know you. Thus, they believe they have rights. It is kind of like the old movie ideology, a vampire cannot come into your house unless you invite them in. But, you, they, everybody has invited them in. And, this is where all of these problems have begun. If you have experienced any, you know they are out there — you know that there are some really messed up people saying and doing some really messed up things. Lying and claiming it to be truth, falsely believing that they know you and, as such, should be able to control you when they have no right to do anything like that at all.

Look to yourself. Are you one those people who believes that you know someone simply because you have read or seen what they have placed on social media or the internet? Are you one of those people who believes that your opinion about a person should be heard so you speak it louder than anyone else? Are you one of those people that believes that you have the right to judge a person even though you have personally achieved nothing of greatness in your own life? Are you one of those people who believes that you actually know a person when you have never met them? Are you a person who feels that they have the right to demand something from another person simply because you are both on the internet?

Like I always say, most people in life are nice and caring. They want to live a good life and they want all others to live a good life, as well. They may like who and what they like, dislike who or what they dislike, but they do not allow their altered sense of internet-based empowerment to guide them down a road of taking inappropriate actions simply because they possess some false sense of self.

In life, at least for those of us in the free world, you can pretty much do anything that you want and you can pretty much say anything that you want. But, these simple facts, lead to many of the greater problems of the whole.

What you do, what you say about others, has wide spanning effects. Therefore, it has to be you who chooses to do and say the right thing and defend those when someone says something bad, wrong, or negative about them in social media or on the internet.

As has been long documented, the people who say or do bad things do it to bring attention to themselves. It is, in fact, one of the quickest ways to gain notoriety. But, just like every stalker, internet or otherwise, who thrives on the acknowledgement of their aberrant deeds, so too should the person of positivity.

Think about when you do something wrong or say something negative, how does it make you feel? If you feel adrenalized, you are surging on the rush of negative emotions. These actions never have positive outcomes and no one ever comes to revere you by saying or doing negative deeds. How do you feel when you say or do something positive? Maybe there is not a big surge of adrenaline but what does occur is a sense of positive empowerment. This is the energy that the world comes to appreciate and revere.

As those who are embarked upon the road to negativity on social media and otherwise probably do not read this blog or blogs like it, they will never hear these words. But, that does not mean they should not be said. For there are those of you who need a reminder that what you are doing, when you are doing and saying something positive, on social media and everywhere else, does make a difference. It does make the world better. Stand up for the better.

As for social media, personally, I don't need the melodrama, so I don't participate. But, if you are good, good will always seek you out. When you see or hear the negative, say or do something positive and then leave the scene of the crime. Leave the negative to wallow in their negativity while the positivity embellishes you.

Bad is always bad. Negative is always Negative. Good is always good. Positive is always Positive.

The good and the positive is always better than the bad and the negative.

I Said Yes When I Should Have Said No
24/06/16 07:47

Has there ever been a situation in your life when you decided to do something and then you realized it was a major mistake — that it really messed up your everything? Most life choices and the events that they lead to are not that dramatic. But, some life choices lead to a completely altered sense of your everything.

In some cases, life changing choices are made and they immediately come to affect the next set of circumstances in your life. In other cases, these choices take much longer to materialize a new and worsted reality in your life. In either case, you are left wondering, *"Why did I decide to do it?"*

People have all kinds of reasons for doing what they do. We all hope that the people we let into our lives are kind, good-spirited, and wish us and the rest of the world well. We meet them, we may like them, we may love them, then we make a choice to do something with them. Interacting with nice, good people, seems to be the right thing to do. What could go wrong?

On the other side of the coin, there are those people who were either born or grew up to be bad, cruel, jealous, angry, uncaring, emotionally out of control, and/or hateful. These people spend their entire existence saying bad things, doing bad things, and attempting to hurt the reality of others. These are the people that, most of us, try to avoid. But, just look at our prisons, they are full of people who embrace this lifestyle and/or were pulled into it by making a choice to interact with one of these of people and were then set on a course to do bad things.

Good, kind actions are obvious. Bad, hateful actions are obvious. All people's lives are born from the thoughts they think, the words they speak, giving birth to the reality they live, and what they do to other people. Though most of us try to seek out only the good, unfortunately we all will encounter the bad and they will, in some cases, force themselves into our lives.

All of these factors give birth to the choices we make. Once made, good or bad, we are the one left dealing with the outcome of these choices.

Choices that alter our life can be small but they can have big effects. Perhaps one of the most obvious of life altering choices, that people make everyday is, give into the desire for sex based upon momentary lust and/or big love. They have sex, they get pregnant, and then their entire everything is instantly changed — all by the action of one choice. Think how many abortions this choice has led to. Think how many children who were born to unfit or unready parents, that totally messed up that child's life, that this choice has created. Though religious teachers will tell you the reason that sex feels so good is so that people will procreate and continue the world's population, this does not take into consideration all the lives that were created and then destroyed simply because someone gave into the choice of sex.

But choice, and the effect it can have, goes to many other realms of personal reality, as well. Each minute of each day, you personally decide to behave in a specific manner. How you behave is a choice. This chosen behavior sets an entire course of events into motion in your life. It creates the people you will meet, how you will interact with them once you have met them, it even creates the next step in your karma because what you say or do sets your everything into motion.

As stated, we all prefer to meet people who are nice and caring. But, has meeting nice people always been the case in your life? Probably not. I am sure you have met people who were just the opposite or those who hid who they truly were on the inside by covering it up with a veil of illusion.

People attract people of like mind. Those who are good and kind find those who are good and kind. Those who are just the opposite are sucked into the illusion offered by the aberrant. But, once you find a person, once you interact with a person, your life then becomes defined by the choice(s) you make while interacting with that person.

If you speak words and do things that will hurt people, what do you think will be the ultimate outcome of your life? You must make a choice. If you choose to do thing that make yourself greater while making other people look lessor, what do you think will be the ultimate outcome of your life? You must make a choice. If you do physical things, based upon physical desire, what do you think will be the ultimate outcome of your life? You must make a choice. If you spend money you don't have, what do you think will be the ultimate outcome of your life? You must make a choice. If you do self-motivate things and just don't care about the consequences to others, what do you think will be the ultimate outcome of your life? You must make a choice.

There is no way that any of us are going to get through life without making a choice that we later realize was a mistake. Whether it was a choice to be in a relationship, associate with a specific person or group, buy something, move somewhere, take a specific job, or do something that later turned out to be a major mistake and/or catastrophe, the small choices you make, in this moment, are the choices that have the potential to come to define the rest of your life. Thus, you really must begin with yourself; for how you think, what you say, what and how you do it, is all a choice. It is your choice. This is why it is understood that all spirituality begins with you. You are the one to make the choice. Therefore, place yourself in a life-situation when you are mentally prepared, in a positive manner, so that you will make the best choices that you can, do the best things that you can, in any given moment. ...Choose well.

*   *   *

23/06/16 18:47

People who are mad at themselves and angry about where they find themselves in life always seek out someone else to focus their anger upon.

Just as those who are self-content and fulfilled are always the ones with a smile on their face and willing to lend a helping hand.

* * *

23/06/16 18:23

If you are looking for the flaws in someone, they are easy to find. But, if you are discussing the flaws in someone else that means that you don't want people to look to closely at your own.

* * *

23/06/16 17:30

If you spend your time hating, being angry, or focusing negative energy, thoughts or words at a person, that individual becomes your source of life-inspiration, thus they control you. Do you want a person whom you hate to control you?

*   *   *

23/06/16 17:21

How long does the pain last for?

* * *

23/06/16 17:21

If you look to others for your inspiration you will forever be disappointed. You can't create what they have created, you can only create what you can create.

* * *

23/06/16 17:20

To know the answer is the ultimate quest but every answer reaches a different conclusion.

*   *   *

22/06/16 08:37

How can you discredit a person who doesn't care what his or her credits are?

Fading Away
22/06/16 07:42

    Have you ever gone somewhere a lot like a bar, a nightclub, a gym, a yoga class, or even a church and you would see the same person there all the time and then you began to see them less and less until you no longer saw them at all? Even online, have you ever witnessed a person postings all the time and then they slowly stop posting as much until they finally stopped posting altogether? You wonder, *"What happened to them? Why are they no longer there anymore?"* What happened is, they moved along, they found a new life that was more important to them than the unfocused life they were previously living trying to make something out of nothing.
    In life, we each seek purpose. We seek to be something, do something, and be a part of something. Many people have no focused talent. Meaning, that there is not something they specifically want to be like a folk singer, a rock star, an actor, a novelist, an artist, a body builder, a black belt, an architect, a rabbi, a school teacher, a military professional, or anything else that takes a lot of focus. Some people just want to exist without trying too hard, yet they still want something to do and something to belong to. This abstract something, within the nothing, is oftentimes the place where people launch into a life that is lived in less than an ideal fashion.
    There are all these things out there that we can find to occupy our time. Some of them are fun and interactive. Some of them are bad for our bodies like bars. Some our good for our bodies like gyms or yoga classes. But, the fact is, when people have nothing they seek something. When they have nothing better to do they seek something (anything) to do. The internet provides this right from the comfort of your own home or right in front of you wherever you are. Some people love to get into twitter wars or battles

on the various other sites. But, what does that equal? It equals nothing, just the opinion of no one floating in cyberspace. Some people actually make a name for themselves by doing something very creative on some site that a vast number of people actually come to like. But, these are generally the people who do actually have a vision for their life. They are consciously doing something as opposed to unconsciously doing nothing.

But, these people, in some cases, also fade away. Why? Because they found something better to do with their life. Something that they consider more important.

Generally, when people walk away from the nothing, they have found the more inclusive something. They met someone and fell in love. They had a baby; which is the most essentially important thing anyone can do — raise that child right. They found a good a job that take up all of their time and focus. Maybe they even found religion. But, whatever it was, it was something more than before. Thus, they are gone.

In life, we all reach these moments. A time when we leave the, *"That,"* behind for the, *"This."* It's natural.

Sometimes we are forced into this decision. Sometimes it is slow progress that is gained through time and new understandings. Whatever the cause, it happens to pretty much everyone. Sure, you can find the old-timer who has been sitting at the same bar stool forever. But, even they eventually will die. Then, the forced realization comes at the ultimate cost.

The main thing to keep in mind is that when it is time for a person to move along, let them move along. Don't hold them bound to who they used to be simply because you never want them to change because you haven't changed. …You haven't, at least not yet. But, you will eventually change too. Then what? Do you want to be held back?

Life moves along. Let it change when it changes. Let people change when they change. Let them fade away when they decide it is time to fade away.

What is Their Motivation?
21/06/16 16:09

I believe that one of the key factors that people overlook when they engage in interpersonal relationships is that they do not question a person's motivation for doing what they do. They may meet a person or come to interact with them is some way and then they simply take that person at face value. They never question why that person is doing what they are doing, why they are saying what they are saying, and why they are behaving the way in which they are behaving. From not questioning these elemental personality-based life-factors many people are lead down a dangerous road and end up lied to, cheated, hurt, stolen from, and/or generally messed over in life by another person.

People are essential who they are. They are the person they were as a child. They are the person that the child transitioned into and became an adult.

The various factors that come to shape a child, define that person as an adult. Some people advance through the varying stages of human consciousness, as they move from childhood to adulthood, while others are lost and locked into the emotions of their childhood.

The people who are angry adults were made so in their childhood. The people who lie, cheat, steal, lash out, hurt, and deceive others learned these habits in their childhood. People who are enraged adults; those who go, *"Postal,"* are those who never learned proper, enlightened control over their emotions. People who hurt people as an adult do so because they were hurt as a child and no one ever said, *"I'm sorry,"* and fixed the damage that was done to them.

We are what we were schooled to be.

The problem with this truth is, however, as people grow through life; as people get older, many learn how to hide their True Self from the world. They hide who they truly are until they are in a close relationship with another person or they find a person that they want something from, then the gloves come off and the damage is instigated.

But, the fact is, if a person simply studies why a person is doing what they are doing — what is their motivation for doing what they are doing, then many a damaged life could have been prevented.

The simply answer to this quandary is, if a person's motivations aren't completely obvious to you simply ask, *"Why do you do what you do? What do you hope to achieve by doing what you do? What do you want from me? And, why do you behave as you behave?"*

But, the fact is, many people have become consummate liars as they pass through life. They may be horrible human beings on the inside but they are great lairs on the outside. So, sometimes it is hard to know who is what. But, you still need to look and question.

As I often discuss the various realms of spirituality in this blog and in my other writings, I go back to the fact that, in my life, I have met a number of false, so-called, spiritual teachers. These people should be ashamed of themselves for claiming to be spiritual and/or in their teaching anything. But, due to whatever it was they encountered in their childhood and their low sense of esteem and accomplishment in their adulthood, they turn to teaching spirituality in order to make themselves feel whole. This, while they live an aberrant lifestyle and cannot even control their own desires and emotions. And, the control of personal desires and emotions is at the heart of all spiritual transcendence. If they can't do that, then how do they claim to be a spiritual anything? As I frequently state, people can get away with this because there is no required credential to claim spiritual knowledge. Sad, but true. Thus, people are allowed to lie about who and what they truly are.

On the other side of the issue I have also met people who truly embrace their spirituality. They leave their ego in check, live a humble lifestyle defined by meditation and prayer. They go out of their way to help everyone that they can and never even think to charge a dime for their services. This is true spirituality. Working on one's self while helping all-others before ever stepping up to the pulpit.

But, here's the fact, most people don't care about spirituality. They are not going to go looking for a spiritual teacher. For these people, they are not going to be impacted by these false prophets. So, my warning means nothing to them. And, that's a good thing. But, there are a million self-motivated people doing self-motivated things out there. They are going after what they want and they hurt people as they do it and they do not care. This is why you need to study a person's motivations before you ever come to interact with anyone on anything more than a superficial level.

Some people's motivations are obvious. They want to make money off of you. They want to know you. They want to use you for what you know. They want to go out with you. They want to have sex with you. And, the list goes on... But, you have to be personally aware enough, and care enough about what happens next in your life, to not let yourself fall prey to a person with less than ideal intentions. You need to be able to look at a person and see their motivations.

On the more physical side of things, there is the guy in the nightclub trying to pick up on the girl. He knows what he's doing and the girl knows what he's doing. Maybe she likes what she sees, maybe she doesn't. But, this is the play of life. The motivations are obvious. Most of life is not like this, however.

Then, there is the other side of the issue... For example, I think back to this one time that my friend Venchinzo and I had gone to *The Rainbow* on Sunset. We were upstairs in the small dance floor area enjoying our drinks while listening to the music. This one really tall, dirty looking, long haired guy kept rubbing his body on this tiny Latina girl. She was really cute, dressed in a flowing white miniskirt dress. I liked what she was wearing but she looked very out of place as this was in the height of the hair metal days. The guy kept going up on her and she kept trying to move away. The loser wasn't paying attention to her wishes to leave her alone. So, I went up and shoved him back. I told him to, *"Back off!"* He did listen to me and that was good thing because I wasn't playing — I wasn't about to have any of that forced action taking place on a young helpless girl in my presence.

…Don't you hate that when losers come up and try to force their attentions on you and/or other people? It's happened to me and I don't like it.

Anyway, the girl was very appreciative of what I did. We had a drink, danced, and the night went on for a time. Then, the guy she came with, this aging rock star, who had a couple of other young girls in tow, decided it was time to have pizza, which they serve downstairs. The reservation for his table was ready. The girl ran up to me and invited Venchinzo and me along. Sure… Why not… We went downstairs and tried to join the party. The guy, being a total dick was complaining about the money it would cost if we ate and drank with them. *"But, he saved me,"* the girl exclaimed. Obviously, the guy wasn't aware enough about anything and he did nothing, leaving it to me to take care of his date. But, I just didn't need the bullshit. I reached into my pocket and threw a hundred-dollar bill down on the table and said, *"Here. The pizza's on me."* Venchinzo and I went back upstairs. Sad, because I liked the girl. But, I got it. He was an aging rock star and for some reason people are always infatuate with that.

Okay, okay… Why am I telling this story? Let's look to motivations…

The young girl, out at a nightclub. Remember how fun that was when you were in your early twenties? The jerkoff guy who was bothering her, a total loser, couldn't get a girl by asking her to dance so he had to go rub up against them on the dance floor. Me, I like girls and I'm not afraid to fight. In fact, I used to love to fight. So, that kind of shit is not going to go down in my presence. The young girl, she appreciated my standing up for her. Maybe she like the way I looked, maybe she liked me, I don't know? But, we were on our way to having our moment. Venchinzo, he was drunk, so he didn't care. The aging rock star; well… He was an aging rock star… He had been there once and I'm sure, in his mind, he still was someone or something. So, I get it… What was his was his; i.e.: the girls he had in tow; at least for that night. He didn't want two guys, way younger than him, honing in. He called out the only thing he could, the price of the pizza. Personally, I think that made him look like a loser. But, as it turned out, the pizza was on me.

Never saw the girl again. Though I wished I would have. I'm sure she has lived her life… But, did she think about it? Did she think about living her life? Did she study her life? Did she study the motivations of people in her life? Or, did she just haphazardly end up where she ended up? I imagine the ladder is the case, as that is what most people do.

So, here's the point, are you mindful enough to study the motivation of people you interact with? In the past, have you? If you have not, has there been negative outcomes from some of your interaction? If you have studied a person's motivations before becoming involved with them, what was the outcome in that case? Positive or negative?

Life is about opening your eyes. In fact, enlightenment is about opening your eyes and seeing the truth in all things.

So, how do you live your life? Are your eyes opened, studying everything? Or, do you live in a cloud-filled haze, simply reacting to all that you encounter be it bad or good?

My suggestion, open your eyes, don't let people fool you. Study the motivation for why they are doing what they are doing. From this, I believe you will live a better life.

* * *

21/06/16 08:54

Who were you in your past life?

Who cares?

If past lives do exist, that was then, this is now.

All you have is the now of the life you are living.

*   *   *

21/06/16 07:20

Most people don't want to know the truth.

They don't want to know the truth about themselves, about what they believe, about the way their actions have negatively affected others, and about how people truly feel about them.

If you hide from the truth, you are living a lie. This makes you a liar.

The truth or the lies, your choice.

*   *   *

20/06/16 17:12

How many lies have you believed?

*   *   *

20/06/16 16:56

Just because somebody says something does not make it the truth.

Is everything you say the truth?

Are your words based upon facts?

Are your words based upon your beliefs?

Are your words based upon conjecture?

Or, are your words predicated upon the way you want people to view you?

If you've ever told a lie then that makes you a lair.

What karma do you think unfolds due to the telling of lies?

What you say to the world sets the stage for your entire life.

* * *

20/06/16 16:03

Notoriety without accomplishment is meaningless.

What You Say You Do
20/06/16 09:12

Life is a very complex, complicated path of action and reaction. What you say, what you do affects not only your everything but everyone else's everything, as well. People don't seem to realize this, however. They say what they say, they do what they do, and then they live their life believing that what they are saying, what they are doing, is okay. They do this until they reach a point in their life when their life is not going in the direction that they had hoped or they run into the wall of reality and see that what they have said, what they have done has not only negatively affected those they said and did things to but irreconcilably damaged has been done to their own life, as well.

What makes you think that you can do anything you want? What makes you think that you can say anything you want about anybody? Do you not believe that your words, your actions, and even your thoughts have far reaching consequences? If you don't, or if you don't care, you really need to rethink your life and lifestyle.

I speak of this a lot but there are a certain group of people who are attracted to negative speech. If someone is voicing something antagonistic about someone there is a certain type or person who will congregate around that individual and cheer them on. There is adrenaline in hatred. But, think about it, these people may be cheering a single figure on, making that person feel empowered but what are these people doing with their own life? Are they making the world a better place? No, they are simply finding a place to enhance and actualize their anger. Do you think that is right: psychologically, physiologically, or otherwise?

Negativity only breeds negativity. Anger only breeds anger.

At the sourcepoint of all things in this life, there is one person saying or doing one thing. What they say or do has wide spanning consequence. But, as stated, most people do not think about this.

These wide spanning consequences go from small events caused by small people to very large events instigated by a single person. But, anything negative is negative. Say or do something negative, small or large, and the consequences will be negative.

I am sure if you look to events in your own life, whether is was a situation on the school yard, at your work, in your relationship(s), or in the whole of your greater life, you will be able to remember an occurrence that took place and understand that the small things a person has said about you or done to you have affected your larger everything. Personally, I think back to a situation that occurred in my own life. I had meet this girl, she was beautiful and we were totally into each other. She had previously gone through addictions, rehabs and stuff, so I knew she wasn't fully functioning, but love is love, you overlook all the flaws. One of the first things she said, when I was meeting with some of her friends for the first time was, "His life has been messed up before, now I am going to totally destroy it." This was meant as a joke. Everybody, but me, laughed, though I did provide one of those pretend smiles. Though she did not set out to intentionally do so, she did destroy my life. Her love was never-ending, but she really messed up my everything.

She said it. She did it. And, my life was never the same.

This is the thing about life… You really must be present in your moment. You really must be conscious of who you allow into your life. And, you really must be willing to cut a person loose, even if you love them, if their pathway is set upon destruction; intentionally or otherwise.

The things a person says, the way a person behaves, the things that a person allows to come into their life, defines their life. These things can be positive and good or they can be negative and bad. What a person says, what a person does, how a person acts, defines who they are. How you feel about them should be seen as simply how you feel about them. As we all understand, emotions come and go, so you should not let your life be defined by them. Especially, if your emotions lead you down a road that will destroy your life.

Ultimately, you must understand life begin with you. What you say, affects everything and everybody. What you do, affects everything and everybody. You may feel momentarily good or empowered by saying or doing something negative but the consequences of your actions will always come back to haunt you.

You are responsible for what you say. You are responsible for what you do. You are responsible for the actions and the reactions your words and actions instigate.

What are you going to say or do next?

I'm an Artist, Goddamn It!
20/06/16 08:27

"I'm an artist, goddamn it! I don't have to rationalize, justify, explain, or defend anything that I do!" This is a bold statement that my Zen Filmmaking brother, Donald G. Jackson and I used to voice whenever we ran into some negativity or controversy about what we were doing. The main thing to know, however, is that this statement was made in fun. We always said it with a smile on our face. I suppose if you read it, this statement comes off as kind of harsh. But, it was not meant to be that way.

It was actually Don who first coined it. But, it became our mutual motto. So, we said it quite often.

Don, more than I, (at least in the early days), received much more criticism for his films and his filmmaking practices. Once he passed away, it became me who was awarded the crown and I became the focus. It is essential to note, however, as has always been the case, there are more people who liked what he and I did than those who did not. But, as also always seems to be the case in life, those who embrace negativity as their primary means of communication, those who look for faults rather than merit, are the most vocal. Wrong, I believe. But, such is life...

Anyway, I believe I put this statement in my book, Zen Filmmaking, and I have been told it was quoted a few times, in various places, by people trying to cast shade on me for writing it. I mean come on... Those people who want to base their lives upon criticism always look for something to criticize. This is true in the film game, in the film watcher game, and everywhere else.

Me, I always question, *"Why?"* Why do you, why does anyone, wish to focus their life in seeking out the flaws instead of looking to the perfection of the process? Why??? The world is beautiful, people are beautiful, artistic creations are beautiful, if you just let them be.

Anyway, this statement really goes to the greater whole of anyone who is following the path of creation and/or art; because, as stated, there will be those people out there seeking out your flaws. If you are an artist, you need to be an artist. You need to create your art as you envision your art. That is what true creativity is all about. And, to anyone who wants to criticize it, screw 'em. Let's see what they have created. And then, let's throw some criticism their direction, see how they respond.

In other words, be strong in your art. Do what you do and not care about what others think. If they are so vocal to have the time to waste, simply talking about other people and other things that has nothing to do with them, that means they are not doing anything worth while with their own life in the first place.

Most People Just Fade Away
20/06/16 07:28

In this age of the internet I believe that most of us are highly aware of the fact of how much information is out there about us and how people can use this information for good and/or negative purposes. It is out there; it must be true; right? Well, yes and no...

As we are in the age of the internet and so many people post so many things about themselves — I mean, just think about all of the selfies that people post everyday. Now, think about, just a few years ago there was no such thing as a selfie but since the rise of first the camera phone and then the smart phone, people put all this stuff out there. And on Twitter... OMG all the nonsense that people put out there. Get a life!

Though this is the case of many people, particularly those of a specific generation, this is not the case for everyone. For example, have you ever searched yourself on the internet? What did you find? What did you think about what you found? But, more importantly, do you ever search someone else? Maybe someone who was a friend from a few years ago but you lost touch? I think most of us have. What did you find? In some cases, you find all kinds of stuff but in other cases they are gone; nothing — vanished from the face of the earth. But, what happened to them? Where did they go? Why is there no information about them?

Of course, there could be any number of reasons for this, and there is no need to list them here. But, with nothing, then the thought remains, *"Whatever ever happened to them?"* An answer you will probably never find.

The fact is, in life, most people pass between birth and death and leave no remnants. The only additive to this life-space they may leave behind is their children. Certainly, in this space and time in history more people are probably going to be cast out there to infamy and/or immortality in cyberspace but this is a new phenomenon only a couple of decades deep. Think back thirty years, getting your name, *"Out there,"* was almost impossible. If you did not find a publisher for your books or articles, a record company for your music, a producer to put you in a film, or go through enough school to gain an advanced degree and were then hired to teach by a university your world identity was zero. Now, everybody self-publishes, self-produces, and claims to be a teacher and/or knower of whatever. So, for better or for worse, they get their name out there. They get it out there with no buffer zone, no editing, and no vetting process. Like I said to a friend yesterday, when we were at this event and I had to keep getting out of the way of these two people with cameras trying to take a photograph of me, *"Just because you own an expensive camera does not mean that you are a photographer."*

But, back to the point, pretty much everybody is out there. They are something and somebody. At least in their own mind. But, some are not. They are gone, hidden, lost like Zen. I guess the ultimate question that will be lost to only the questioning mind of those who knew them once but no longer, *"Where did they go and what happened to them?"*

Most people just fade away.

* * *

17/06/16 13:26

Some people have the mental-aptitude for change and personal growth. Some do not. Which one are you?

The Words Don't Do It Justice
17/06/16 07:33

Have you ever had the experience when you were telling someone a story about an experience you had and though they heard your words you can tell that they did not even come close to actually understanding the experience? You saw that what you were saying was not penetrating the mind of the person whom you were speaking with and from this maybe you tried to tell the story again, adding a few words, a more in-depth description, maybe you even added why you did what you did and how you were feeling at that moment. But still, nothing. They don't get it.

Communications are based upon a common set of understandings. Communications are based upon the ability of a person to listen to what another person is saying. Communications are based upon what the other person has experienced and the predetermined projections that they place upon the person to whom they speak. In other words, people have their minds made up from the moment they meet a person. In some cases, they are open enough to actually listen to what the other person has to say and perhaps learn and grow from that individual's set of experiences. In other cases, their mind is locked. They have made up their mind. They judge everything, everyone, and every word from what they already believe and that is that.

In life, we meet people. In life, we are both forced to speak with people and choose to speak with people. In life, we present our set of experiences to others in the hopes that they will come to better understand us, what we have lived through, and what we believe.

Some people are outspoken and try to force their experiences and beliefs onto others. If the other person or persons are not listening or are not understanding, they simply keep rehashing the same subject over-and-over again. Most, are not like that, however. They tell their story, maybe alter or enhance it once or twice, but when it is not being heard, silence is embraced understanding that the other person is never going to understand.

As you pass through life there will be those that will develop a deep communicative understanding with you. As you pass through life there will be those who will never truly understand anything that you say. You can choose to re-state and re-phrase or you can choose to simply let it go. And, this is perhaps one of the hardest states of inter-human communication for when you have chosen to tell someone a story you want them to understand. But, the fact is, some will not — they never will no matter how much you try to explain and re-explain. Thus, when telling your story has failed, silence is your only mindful option.

*   *   *

17/06/16 07:11

It is easy to dismiss, disregard, and even critique and criticize what a person is feeling. It is much harder to actual care and set about upon a course to make them feel better.

How Closely Do You Listen?
16/06/16 07:25

For anyone who knows me they know that for distraction I like to go to Thrift Shops and Antique Stores, finding, as I like to put it, *"Unique pieces of cultural memorabilia."* Most of the time, I find nothing. And, the people who shop there, most of them I don't want to know. But every now and then...

Today I was down in this shop in Santa Ana and I came across this vintage turntable. The serial number dates it to about '74. It was the top of the line back then.

Not that I need another turntable, because I have several of them, but this one really caught my eye. The interesting thing about it is that it has its previous owner name and social security number etched into it.

Back in the 70s they used to sell these metal etchers. They told the world it was a way to protect your possessions and provide the police with a way to find them if they were ever stolen. That, of course, was long before identify theft and all that kinds of stuff. This guy, (I imagine he is dead), but there is his name and social security number, etched onto the unit, protecting his possession.

Anyway, I get it home and I hook it up to my vintage Marantz Quad power amp. A, *"Quad System,"* was the way deep predecessor to 5.1 and stuff like that. Supposedly, the big brother and the next evolution to Stereo. But, kind of like DAT, (though it was, in fact, way better), it never really took off. You do have a Sony DAT recorder don't you?

Plugged in, I put on Iggy Pop's *Zombie Birdhouse* LP. It sounded great! I later also put the same record on my main, Audio-Techinca turntable hooked up to my 5.1 system and though 5.1 is great, the vintage system just sounded way better.

This is the thing that many people do not understand and/or don't care about. Sound; particularly music: the way it is recorded, what it is recorded with, and what it is played back upon truly creates vast differences in the soundscape. This is why so many true musicians harken back to the old analog mixers and record on actual tape with vintage tape recorders to create their music. The sound is just better.

Do you ever take the time to really listen? Do you ever take the time to really study the sound? For audiophiles like me, I do it all the time. (And, I am smiling as I write this because it makes me sound like such an elitist, which I am not). But really, do you ever study the sound? Do you ever just listen? Do you ever compare the subtleties of the sound: whenever and wherever you are?

Most people just talk. And, they talk too much. Most people never listen to their voice, they never control their voice, and they never care about who hears their voice as they feel they have something worth saying. Let's be honest, most people don't. The world would be a better place if they said nothing at all. Voice(s) invade the sound-space of silence.

We are all bombarded with sound, especially those of us who live in a city. Some places like Hong Kong vibrate with ambient sound 24/7. It can be really maddening if you don't live some place where you can shut it out. Some people that live around us talk too loud, play their music too loud, or rev their engines too loud. Construction, that is just a life killer.

We are all sounded by sound. We are all forced to listen to sound. But, the sound we choose, (the sounds you choose), do you ever take the time to listen for the subtleties? Do you ever listen for the silence between the notes?

Sound is a very unique thing. It produces very unique effects in our life. What you hear shapes your life. What do you hear? Do you listen for the subtleties within the sound?

*   *   *

16/06/16 07:25

People with messed up lives try to mess up the life of others.

**There is Always Some Reason
to Find Someone to Hate**
15/06/16 08:57

With the shootings that took place in Florida constantly in the news right now, it is hard not to think about how this type of attack-violence has become the new normal. It is everywhere and it is growing. This is not the first time this style of attack has taken place and sadly it will probably not be the last.

As I have spoken about recently, there is always one person doing the do in these incidences. In some cases, just like the gangbanger in street warfare, there is a group of people egging a person on. But, at the root of all evil, there is one person doing one thing.

I suppose in some cases these people believe that they can get away with their actions. But, in this new technologically based world, where there are cameras everywhere and highly advanced forensic sciences, they should know they will be caught. But, I suppose many are willing to die for their religious ideology and they do not care. They don't care until they get caught and get put into prison. Then, good luck. But, that is not the point.

People do bad things. People do bad things to people that should not have bad things done to them and this has been going on forever. All the murders, all the lynchings, all the rapes, all the beatings, all the verbal assaults, and the list goes on and on. People do bad things and they justify their actions in their own mind. In most case, the people who do this stuff would clearly be seen as mentally ill but they seek no help. This is why prisons are full and there is a world full of a populous that has been victimized and are traumatized for life.

For a person to seek mental counseling they have to be self-aware enough to know that what they are thinking, feeling and/or the way they are acting is wrong. The problem is, many people with psychological issue; be this an advanced psychiatric illness like psychosis or schizophrenia or a biochemical or mood disorder simply act out, they do what they do and then they either blame the person or persons they are acting out upon or they are so lost in their own mind and their own sense of self that they blame no one at all. They certainly never blame themselves.

People can easily find a person to hate. In some cases, this hated may be brought on by what a specific individual has done to a specific person but in most cases this anger is simply cast to the masses that inhabit a specific race or group.

As I have discussed in the past, I grew up in a racially charged world where many people hated me simply because I was white. So, I experienced racism from the other side of the norm. Violence was everywhere around me and I had to constantly be on guard, which undoubtedly was part of the causation factor that lead to the chronic anxiety syndrome I began to suffer from in my teenage years. I was horrible. Someday I will probably tell the story. But, it was bad. I too, as a young person with no personal finances and a family that was obviously to what I was going through, could not seek out mental help. So, I suffered. As such, I get it why people don't seek the help they need. This is the sad case of the world. But, the people who are unleashing these violent acts are adults. I could say they should have the mental aptitude to seek out help but instead they turn their focus to those who embellish and cultivate their mental disorder and ultimately guide them towards violence.

When I was young I saw how I was simply categorized by my race. People always called me racial slurs. These young people had obviously learned these terms and this style of behavior from their older family members or parents. My parents and family members also defined people by racially orientated definitions. So, I grow up unintentionally learning that was the way you defined a person whenever you were angry with them and/or you didn't like them. Wrong, yes. But, this is societal programming. This is what people are taught everyday.

Everyone who wasn't you or yours was that. And, *"That,"* was always something to be looked down upon. Think about how many people are schooled and programmed into this train of thought everyday, not just about race but about personal lifestyle choices and everything else.

This is life and this is how people are taught to behave. In this modern world, the masses, on the larger scale, have certainly become more accepting. But, again, damage occurs when one person is doing one thing and this is where all the problems begin. If the person who is setting about on a course to hurt others would first seek out help, they probably could be helped. But, the fact is, they do not. And, there is oftentimes a reason for this.

People can't get help because they either do not possess the mindset to understand that they need help or they cannot afford the help they would get if they could pay for it. Yes, there are free clinics and stuff like that. But, they are generally horrible places that no one except the person who is so mentally aware that something is truly going wrong with them would even think about going to. But, most people, especially those with psychiatric or psychological conditions are not that engaged. Not to mention all the societal stigma that is still attached to seeking out psychological counseling. Thus, people grow up indoctrinated into disliking or hating other races, other religions, other sexes, or other lifestyles. From this, in association with untreated psychological disorders, murder is unleashed onto the world.

So, what can be done about this? People hate people because they do not approve of their race, their lifestyle, their thoughts, their behavior, or their actions. People hate counties like the U.S. because it is a bully and tries to stick its nose in the business of other countries and force-guide their political systems. But, whether it is the U.S., the political system of some other country, a group of bangers that doesn't like the gang on the next block, or simply a person who doesn't like you, people act out in inappropriate ways. The source is them. Thus, the source is also you.

What do you do? How do you act? How do you behave? Does what you do instigate the anger of others? Do you call out to the masses, *"Look at me. Accept who I am!"* Or, can you be silent in your own self awareness?

There are a lot of people doing a lot of good things out there: doctors, nurses, psychologists, and the farmer who grows the food that you eat. What are you doing to make things in this world better? Are you going to school to learn a trade that can actually make a positive difference to the world? Or, are you just embellishing the lifestyle of what you think should be right by diminishing all that you believe to be wrong?

Here is the key, if you think something is wrong and if any action you take to remedy that wrong hurts anyone or anything, you are the one that is wrong. If you behave in a manner that hurts anyone, you are wrong.

Is what you are doing, how you are acting, what you are saying hurting someone? Then your actions are wrong.

Who are you to believe that you have the credentials to tell anyone how to behave? Who are you to believe that you have the credentials to be empowered enough to decide to hurt someone else for who or what they are? If you believe you are knowledgeable enough or empowered enough to take any negative action towards any person than you should really seek out help. Help, that will change your mind.

Good is always good. Good hurts no one.

The One at the Center Point
14/06/16 07:49

As I alluded to in the blog of yesterday, there is one person who is responsible for whatever actions take place in life. There is one person who is the center-point and the source-point. These actions may be good and positive, they may be unthinking and uncaring, or they may be consciously set to hurt and disrupt the life or lives of others. Whatever mindset is employce, there remains one person who is the responsible party.

To tell a story...

I had a meeting up on Melrose yesterday. It was an overcast, cloudy June day in L.A. Now, they call it, "June gloom." I don't know who came up with that title but all the weather people use it. But, that's okay with me. I like cool, overcast days.

The main thing I noticed as I drove up from the South Bay was that there was so little traffic. I got on the 405 and I did not encounter one single traffic jam. This, on a Monday, which is usually very crowded. I got off the freeway and drove north on La Cienega. It was the same, no traffic. Amazing, it was like driving in L.A. twenty years ago before so many people moved in.

Due to the lack of traffic, I had some time so I grabbed my favorite breakfast over at *The Original Framer's Market:* a Belgium waffle with fresh strawberries and whipped crème and a latte; non-fat, of course. Afterwards, I was still on the good side of time so I took a quick walk around *The Grove*.

Back on my way, I did my meeting and I was again on the move.

I was driving down Melrose. Now, for those of you or may or may not know, Melrose was a hot spot in the

1980s. It was a cultural epicenter. There were tons of great shops, where you could get some great clothes, and all the young and the trendy hung out. The 80s were great but they ain't ever comin' back. Now, it's just a bunch of shops, restaurants, and people attempting to seek out the remnants of another era that is no longer here.

In any case, as I was driving down the street, one of those double decker Hollywood tour, tourist bus was driving up ahead. It stopped, looking at some celebrity or location or something. Immediately, some tourist guy, in his tourist rent-a-car, slams on his breaks right next to the bus to see what they were seeing. By doing this, in essence, he shut down Melrose Ave. People in the cars behind me were yelling and honking but nothing… This guy decided that he was going to do what he was going to do and the rest of the world be damned.

I sat there in disbelief. I never behave like that. Behind the wheel or otherwise I always try to take other people and other people's lives into consideration. But, most people are not like that. They only care about what they care about and here (this) is the sourcepoint for all of the world's problems. People decide to desire something that no one else cares about and they alter and destroy the lives of others while they unconsciously and uncaringly do what they do.

This style of selfish action can make some people get angry, like the drivers of the cars behind me. It can make blood pressure go up. It can even cause violence. Who is to blame? In this case, the person who parked their car in the middle of a thoroughfare, not thinking of anyone but himself. But, as stated, whatever the circumstance, all life problems are created by one person doing one thing. You can always find the culprit.

This is an important point to keep in mind as you pass through life. Who are you doing what you are doing for? And, how is what you are doing affecting others? If what you do affects anyone in anyway you are responsible for all of the repercussions. Do you want to be responsible for repercussion in your life? And, do you care? If you don't care, that says a lot about you. Because you really should care.

As there is one person who is the sourcepoint for every ever-expanding life action, you are the sourcepoint for who and what you encounter and what comes next in your life. What you do not only affects you it affects everything, everybody, everywhere around you.

What are you going to do next?

* * *

14/06/16 07:15

You can't tell anyone anything unless they are willing to listen to what you have to say.

Death, Religion, and Psychological Abnormalities
13/06/16 13:40

With the recent mass-shooting that took place in Florida over the weekend, the minds of the masses are again focused on terrorism. Though the term, *"Terrorism,"* is a common way to categorize the killings of others, at least in this instance, there was one person to blame. And, one person is generally the one-person who kills others.

If we look to recently history, whenever one of these events takes place, all eyes and emotions are focused on that event. Whether it was the London bombings, the Paris shootings, the Mumbai hotel attack, the Bali explosion, or the mother of all terrorist attacks, 911, at the core of these events is one person doing one thing. Yes, in some cases there are a group of people who coalesce but any group is made up of individual minds that make a choice to do some thing for some reason.

In these modern days, the Islamic religion is claimed to be the sourcepoint for most of these attacks. Though many will argue that true Islam would not condone these actions, there is, none-the-less, those who lay claim to Islamic teachings and promise divine salvation to all those who partake. The fighter pilots who were titled the, "Kamikaze," were no different. They were willing to die for their emperor who was believed to be divine. The Christians of The Crusades, no different. And, the list goes on. We, of thinking minds, have to question who could possibly believe that killing would lead to the divine paradise of heaven (by whatever name you call it)? But, many buy into this. They buy into it just as the gangbangers who kill people on the streets are willing to spend their life in jail once they get caught.

Let's not forget, here in American, there are about ninety handgun murders a day. Most have noting to do with religion, just someone attempting to gain control over another. So, the fifty or so who died this weekend are a small number compared to what goes on day-to-day. And, this says nothing about all of the murders and all of tragedies that take place on a daily basis across the globe.

You can claim religion if you want to. But, again, at the source of all inhumanity is one person doing one thing.

Religion is almost a scapegoat. *"They did it because they were religious."* Wrong, they did it because they were psychologically messed up and they sought out religion as an excuse.

Have you ever encountered someone who was really psychologically messed up? Hopefully you haven't and never will because they have the potential to really mess up your life, but I have. They may appear to be normal on the outside, but when no one is looking they are screaming like a banshee, unable to control their emotions. I have written about some of my encounters with people of this nature in previous blogs, in years gone past, and in other places. But, the fact is, many of them claim religion. Why do they do this? Because it is an abstract science where they can say anything. There is no certification they must possess to say what they say and do what they do. They can claim holy scripture as their source or they claim personal realization but it all leads to the same sourcepoint; they are not normal. They do not fit in. If they were normal, if they could fit in, they would not turn to these abstract sciences to justify their existence.

The fact is, the majority of these people are biochemically imbalanced. But, they are not self-aware enough to go and get medicated and stay medicated. In other words, they lie to themselves while justifying their own self-definition. Which means, they are simply wrong. They are not aware enough to be aware, yet they walk among us and unleash horrific acts that ruin the lives of many people.

Do these people ever take their biochemical imbalance and/or insanity to the place where they help people instead of hurting them like say Sri Ramakrishna did? No, they simply use whatever they believe as a way to make themselves feel a part of something and/or gain disciples and/or make money. All while hurting everyone's life they touch because they are not honest and true to other people and/or self-aware enough to be honest and true to themselves. Do they ever say, *"I'm sorry,"* and actually try to fix anything they've broken in another person's life due to their insanity? No, because they are too much in self-denial about the actions they are unleashing. They only want to, *"Do."* And, people deciding to, *"Do,"* is probably the biggest source of catastrophe on this planet.

This world is full of a lot of messed up people. These people do messed up things. They may claim religion as their sourcepoint but if all you unleash is damage there is no holiness in anything you do. You will NOT go to heaven.

Buyer Beware
13/06/16 08:04

Have you ever purchased something that was advertised to do something very specific and when you got it home it was terrible? I didn't work at all. I have…

There is all this, *"As Seen on TV,"* stuff that looks really good when you watch the commercials. Have you ever purchased any of those items? When you get them home are they what you expected or are they made so cheaply that they barely do what you are told they are suppose to do; if they do anything at all?

Though I've never bought anything from the TV adds, now that several stores have the, *"As seen on TV,"* sections I have been lured into a few purchases. They've all turned out to be terrible. They are made so cheaply, not like they appear on TV, and they barely work; if they function at all! Buyer Beware.

This sold on TV stuff is not new. Even back in the early days of cable they were doing it. Back when I used to stay up all night, sometime I would leave my computer, where I was writing something or put down my guitar or step away from the keyboards to sit back with a glass of the grape and watch a little late night TV. Back then, you would see all kinds of stuff that they wouldn't show during the normal watching hours. I so remember this commercial that used to be in rotation where they were selling, *"Actual diamonds, rubies, and sapphires."* And, they were selling them for like $2.00. Of course, I would wonder, *"How."* But, they swore they were real. Though I never purchased one, I am sure many people did. Real, I don't think so. Buyer Beware.

I purchased this tower fan a few years ago. It was really cool. It has all of these controls and a temperature gage to guide it to fan you with cooler temperature; down to like sixty degrees. Plus, it will supposedly filter your air. As a fan it works fine but anything else: cooler temperatures, clearer air; zero. Total false advertisement. Buyer Beware.

I think back a decade or so. A company released this unit that had you put a special pickup on your guitar, hook it up to your Mac, and it would supposedly write out every note that you played. What a great idea! What a great boon for music composition. The only problem was; it didn't work at all! Totally piece of junk. It would occasionally annotate one or two of the notes you played but they were generally wrong. Buyer Beware.

Back in the late 70s they came out with the first portable turners for your guitar. You would plug in your guitar and you could tune your strings to any note you wanted. I rushed out to buy one. I got it home, it didn't work. I tried to take it back the next day to this music shop in Santa Monica and they refused to give me money back. It went back and forth and back and forth. In fact, it was the only time that I got so angry that I actually found myself wanting to cry because I was so pissed that I couldn't just jump over the counter and beat the shit out of the asshole shop owner who sold it to me. This was, of course, before Yelp and stuff like that. I guess I could have taken him to court but I was young and that kind of stuff takes forever and you rarely actually get paid. Buyer Beware.

…At least they came out with better guitar tuners, that actually worked, a short time later.

On the other side of the issue, maybe fifteen years ago, I decided to open up the doors of my martial art organization. It was started back in '79 at a time when it was very hard to get valid martial art rank certification from Korea. And, it has been functioning ever since. But, at the time, (fifteen years ago), I saw a need for a place for people to gain organizational certification and rank advancement. So, we set up portal on the web and I placed somebody in charge. Membership requests jumped very quickly and it went along for while. Maybe a year or so into it, I decided to look over all of the applications that had come in; checking the one's that were approved and the ones that were not. What I found was that so many of the people applying were providing us with fake martial art certificates and false martial art histories and as the person I had handling the application process was from Korea, he didn't have the eye to spot the fakes. I wanted to invalided many of the memberships and rank certificates. Liars!

Though this goes to more of a, *"Seller Beware,"* statement, it shows that deceit, shenanigans, and tomfoolery go on in all directions. I shut down the open portal to the organization.

So, what does this tell us about life? People lie. People embellish. People make false advertisements when they advertise their wares. People want to make money and they do not care about the purchaser. They only care about their bank account.

When you do what you do to make your living, how do you behave? Do you care about the person on the other end? Or, do you only are about yourself and making your bank?

What you do and how you do it defines who you are. It also defines how you see the world and how the world will see you. This, leads to what you will encounter in your life; as what you do, how you do, and what you do or do not do for others, sets the entire melodrama of your life into motion.

I can tell you how I think you should behave. But, it is you who must decide how to behave. When you define you, should the buyer beware?

*   *   *

12/06/16 09:39

Just because that's what you think doesn't mean that's what I think.

Break the Habit
12/06/16 08:52

People develop bad habits. The reason something is considered a, *"Bad habit,"* is because it produces a negative response either to the person performing the action or to others who are forced to deal with the aftermath of one person's actions. Whether this bad habit is something small like biting the finger nails, an addictive bad habit like smoking, onto behavioral bad habits liking acting out in an inappropriately manner, the sourcepoint for each of these bad habits is one person. Thus, there is one source of action being instigated and, therefore, there is one person to blame.

People commonly never take the time to identify, study, and find a reason why they perform a bad habit. Many, never even think about them. Some, simply justify their bad habits. Most, are in denial about their bad habits. Some people point to psychological or cultural influences as the cause of their bad habits. But, no matter what one sites as the cause, there is still one sourcepoint and one person to blame; the person preforming the bad habit them self.

People commonly do not want to take responsibility for what they do and why they do it. They simply want to do it; whatever that, "It," may be. Most, perform their bad habit throughout their lifetime and they do not care about the effective causation they are having. Meaning, they do not care about what they have done and how it has affected others.

Bad habits equal bad things. Overeating equals an unhealthy person who, due to their weight, invades the space of others. Smoking pollutes their world environment is so many ways. Yet, how many people smoke, destroying this world landscape? People drink and take drugs and kill and maim others when they are behind the wheel. People hurt people by the way they behave and act out. All of this, and more, goes to the definition of a bad habit. People do something over-and-over again, yet they never take the time to look at themselves, define why they do what they do, what affect what they are doing is actually having to the lives of others and the world around them, and then take control over it.

Take a look at yourself. Take a few moments and truly study yourself. What bad habits do you have? Take some time and actually write down your bad habits. What are they? Now, take a few more minutes and define what negativity you have caused by performing your bad habits. Have you hurt your own life? Have you hurt the life of others? Finally, what are you going to do about your bad habit? Are you in control of your life to their point that you can put a stop to your bad habits? Or, are you so out of control of your life and your thinking mind that you do not possess the ability to stop?

The main thing to keep in mind is that a habit is a choice. It is your choice. It is you making a choice to do something and/or behave in a certain way.

Who are you? What do you do? Are you in control of your actions or are they in control of you?

Try Meditation. It Works!
11/06/16 11:01

I was at one of those street art faire things today. It was sprinkling this morning, which is great with me. I love the rain. Though this weather is a bit unusual for So. Cal. in June.

In any case, due to the weather, there were very few people yet to arrive at the event. My lady and I were walking around, looking at the various vendors. As we passed by this one booth the lady steps out and says, *"Try meditation."* I looked at her and smiled as we continued to walk. She then exclaims, *"It works!"* She said that with all of the superiority and sense of supreme knowledge that all true believes possess. I joking whispered to my lady, *"I wonder if she's read any of my books?"*

For better or for worse, most of the martial artists out there know my face. Not so much in the world of spirituality. Though I have written more on that subject than the ladder. One way or the other, it's all good with me… But, I believe this lady's actions ideally illustrate the point of how people incorrectly learn, practice, and then present their craft — especially when that craft has to do with the spiritual realms of existence. Most people bring their self, their ego, and their desire to be seen as something more than an average person to the table wherever they find a place to serve their meal of salvation. Though this is the common condition of life, this is the elemental element that must be overcome if one hopes to ascend through the varying realms of consciousness and gain a true understanding of existence.

If you call yourself a teacher, you are never a true teacher. If you claim to have knowledge, you have no knowledge at all. If you claim that you know and if you tell people how to live, all you are is ego driven because you are only speaking from your own sense of self. If you are hocking your spiritual wares in public you are nothing more than a snake oil salesman. The true sage is silent.

The question I pose is, how does one set up a booth and try to sell meditation as a commodity? Mediation is about stepping beyond the realms of Self. It is not about, *"Here I am. I have something to sell you."* It is not about condemnation when some person smiles at you and keeps on walking.

Have you ever encountered one of those salesmen of Jesus on the street corner? They are yelling and screaming about damnation. If you don't kowtow to their proclamations, they will tell you that you will be damn to hell fire forever. Is that true spirituality? No, it is not.

If someone seeks out meditation, they want to learn how to silence their mind and become one with the all. If someone goes to a street faire they are looking for handmade jewelry and crafts. Though a person with a mind focused upon meditation can embrace that mindset anywhere, at any place, at any time; making meditation a commodity diminishes it to the level of the mind of the salesperson trying to make you buy into whatever it is they believe about themselves and whatever technique they are selling.

"Try meditation. It works!" Yes, it does. But, it only works if your mind, your sense of self, and your ego is not involved.

* * *

11/06/16 07:51

Your hot soup will eventually cool down.

In for the Long Haul
10/06/16 08:40

As we pass thorough life we encounter many people. Some turn out to be essential parts of our ongoing evolution and others do not. Some we believe can help us achieve our dreams while others we see as only an obstacle. It is essential to note, however, there is a fine line between someone who can help us and someone who we see as a hindrance. And, this choice between the two is commonly formulated by an untrained mind.

In life, we see something we want and we set about on a course to achieve it. Some people are very fervent in what they want and they go after it with everything they've got. Most people are not like that, however. They may have a desire to be something or achieve something but their process is undefined and sporadic at best, so their dreams are never lived.

When we we want something we place ourselves in an environment where we can find it. This may mean seeking out a teacher, taking a course, or interacting in certain circles where we may meet someone who can help us on our way. In these situations, when we do meet someone who may help us on our quest, we begin to interact with this person in a very specific manner and this is what sets the stage for our ongoing evolution.

The thing that must be kept in mind, however, is that people are ego based creatures. From this, they bring their ego into any relationship. The older the person is, the bigger and more defined their ego. From this, long term interactions with any individual becomes more-and-more difficult as one passes through their life. Meaning, the young are much more accepting and less judgmental then those with age. Therefore, when you desire to do something and you meet someone who may help you achieve it, if you bring an access amount of personal ego into the relationship it may make the interaction very short lived and from this you may never learn what you needed to learn from the person and, thus, you may never become what you actually desired to become.

Becoming takes time. Becoming takes focus. Becoming takes humbleness and self-restraint before you finally develop the knowledge and the understanding to be what you hoped to be so that you can move forward on your own.

Most people never achieve their dreams because they are ego-motivated. Many feel that they are equal to the person they initially sought out for help and guidance and from this ego-based decision making process they choose to leave the relationship before they had the chance to learn the subtleties of what they hoped to learn. Their logic for leaving can be defined by any number of reasons. And, in most cases, these people possess all kinds of self-defined arguments. They may even bad mouth the person of whom they were once the apprentice. But, if they leave via their ego, before their times of study was complete, they do not emerge with the skillset to go out on their own and actually do what they dreamed of doing. Thus, their ego kept them from achieving.

What this means is that if you truly hope to accomplish something you must be willing to put your ego in check. You must be willing to step back and let someone else dominate the situation for a time. Then, once you have learned the craft, through time, you can step forward into your own light and be what you hoped to become.

In my life, two individuals come to mind that came into my life and truly helped become who I wanted to be. Though, interacting with each of them did present a challenge. The first was one of my primary martial arts instructors, Hee Won Yoon. He was a great-great martial arts technician. But, as anyone who has ever been in business with a Korean will tell you, that relationship will be sticky at best. The guy was a problem. But, through years of interaction I truly gained an exacting sense of teaching the martial arts. The other was my Zen Filmmaking brother, Donald G. Jackson. This guy… A psychologically messed-up egomaniac. But, what he did have was a never ending surplus of film financing, without which we could never have made the films that we did.

The point being, there is always a price to pay if you want to achieve. Those who do achieve do so by staying the course, by being in for the long haul. If you allow your ego and your misplaced sense of self-worth to force you from a relationship, that could truly lead to your achievement, then you will never become what you hoped to be.

In other words, you have to control your ego. You may not like some (or all) of the things a person does or the way they behave but you must keep your eye on the bigger picture. You must understand that life is not all about you and how you feel in any given moment. Life is about you learning and then becoming, not about you simply desiring to be something but never truly taking the steps to get there.

What do you want to become? What steps are you taking to get there? If you feel you are already something, what foundations do you have to make your claim?

Foundations are the steppingstone to life. Are you willing to lay yours?

Another Look at the Same Picture
09/06/16 07:23

People fall into patterns in their life. Some of these patterns are good. They help the person focus their life and accomplish what they set out to achieve. Other patterns simply occur by happenstance. They serve no greater purpose and simply cause an individual to become bogged down with their mediocrity.

It is a common emotion in the life of many people that they wish to become something more than they currently are and/or they wish to be doing something different with their life. Though this is almost universally the case, very few people ever have the focus and the forethought to out think the mundane they embrace.

People allow themselves to be trapped. People allow themselves to be dissatisfied. People allow themselves not to try.

As is forever the case, if you have no desire to be anywhere else doing anything else then your life remains in a state of psychological and metaphysical perfection. This, however, is only the case with a select very few.

Most people never take the time to study what they do and why they do it. Yes, they know they must have a job to pay the bills. Yes, they know they must be at their job at a specific time and from this they find a pattern of when they must go to bed, when they must wake up, how much time they have to get ready in the morning, and when they must leave. This style of pattern is structure. And, structure is essential if you want to actualize any physical outcome in your life.

Though they know this structure must be applied if they wish to maintain their level of sustenance, many hate the fact that they must live within the controlling hands of society — that they must do what they must do, the same way, everyday, of their life. Yet, they do nothing to even try to alter anything.

Patterns go far beyond the nine-to-five. They have the potential go to every element of a person's life. Everything that many people do is control by a pattern that they may not even be aware is in existence. What they eat, how they eat it, what they drink and why, what they do in their free time, what they wear, how they wear it, and the list goes on. Think about this this… What do you do everyday? How do you do it? Why do you do it in that way? Watch yourself. Study yourself. Why are you doing what you are doing the way you are doing it?

By doing things the same way day-after-day nothing new is every experienced. No new reality becomes a part of your reality. This is why most people feel very stuck in their life. But, the fact is, even the smallest bit of difference — even the smallest alterations of your patterns can have an evolving effect on making your life less contrived and more experientially vast.

Everyday decide to do something different. Everyday decide to do something new that you have never done before. This, *"New,"* does not have to be something grand. It can be something as simple as changing the way you put on your shoes.

New always equals different. Different always equals new experiences. New experiences always equals new realizations. New realization always equals a more expansive life defined by greater understandings. Do something new.

Who Owes Who What and Why?
08/06/16 14:59

Recently, I've been writing a lot about human interaction and how what one person does sets the stage for what is to happen next in their life and the life of those whom they have focused their energy upon. The truth be told, I often write about and discuss human interaction. I do this because individual choice, and the actions that follow, is what sets the entire world of human interplay into motion. How one person thinks and what one person does, due to what they think, sets the stage for not only their life but the life of all those they encounter.

In life, people do what they do and they behave as they behave for an undisclosed set of personal logic and reasoning. Whatever they think and feel is no one else's business. That is to say it is no one else's business until they make it someone else's business. Once what is going on in their mind affects the life of another person then what they are thinking and doing sets the stage for a world of karma.

Some One does Some Thing then there is one person who becomes responsible and, thus, there is one person to blame.

I think each of us have encountered another person who, by their selfish and unthinking actions, have come to affect our life in some negative manner. I also believe that most of us have encountered another person who has, very consciously, set about on a course to diminish or damage our lives. If a person has performed these actions unconsciously, that means that they are so locked into themselves that they do not even take the time to consider other people before they act. From this, we can surmise that they live their life at such an unconscious level that they are selfishly oblivious to the world around them. And this, becomes the end-all definition of their life. Then, there are those who consciously choose to do something that hurts someone else. Perhaps this is done by casting their judgments towards another person, perhaps it is done by altering the facts of their life and presenting these falsities to the world as truth, perhaps they actually set about to steal something from a person or do them physical or psychological harm. In any case, this again illustrates that a person who behaves in this manner lives their life at a very low level of human consciousness as they actually desire to have a negative effect on the life of another person.

We, as conscious, caring individuals can question, *"Who would do something like that?"* But, if we look around us, even if we look at occurrences in our own life, this type of behavior is everywhere.

In some cases, we are presented with the opportunity to address what a person has done to us directly. Personally, what I have commonly heard from those who did negative things to my life unconsciously is, *"You should have told me,"* or *"I didn't know."* Those are two of the biggest excuses in the human vocabulary. If you are living your life from a place where what you do or how you behave negatively affects the life of others, no one should have to tell you anything. You should already know! Look around you. Does anybody behave like you? No. Thus, there is your definition that you are acting incorrectly.

I have also had people try to turn the tables on me. They do something wrong yet they try to make me look like the valiant. I mean, come on! How unconscious is that?

Who are you? And, what makes you behave in this fashion? Take a look at yourself and your life and own the blame for what you have instigated.

What I have found is that people who behave in this manner live their entire life based upon lies and deceit. Perhaps they even lie and deceive themselves, I don't know? But, what I do know is that they do not possess enough self-respect to step up to the plate and say, *"I have done something wrong. I am sorry. How can I fix it?"* That is what true human consciousness is all about. Owing what you have done and then attempting to fix it, not attempting to shift the blame.

Like I always say, there is one sourcepoint for all human interactions. If you are the sourcepoint and what you have done negatively affects anyone, you should at least be evolved enough to take responsibility for what you have done and not try to shift the blame. I always wonder how people who have done something wrong and then tried to shift the blame would feel if someone exposed their original actions and/or behavior to the world? It is for this reason that I believe all those who either consciously or unconsciously perform negative deeds should own what they have done, not try to cover it up with lies, and try to fix any damage they have unleashed.

Own it! Care about other people enough to care about what you have done and whom you have harmed! Because if you don't, someday, someone will expose your negative action(s) and who you truly are to the world. It eventually happens to every criminal. Then what?

This is how your actions of now lead to your future.

Life starts with one human action. Think about this, what occurred to you today was based upon what you did yesterday. What did you do yesterday and how did it affect you today?

Some people do things to actually hurt someone. To me, these are the lowest of lows as they are consciously setting about on a course that will do damage to another person's life. This may be in the form of words, lies, unkept promises, or actual physical damage. But, if you set about on a course and you are actually trying to hurt another person, what does that say about you and what do you think will be the ultimate outcome of your life? Do you think you can decide to do damage to another person, no matter what your motives may be, and come out unscathed? No one does… Look at the thieves, the frauds, the liars, and the cheats of the world, where do they end up? Look at the criminals of the world, what becomes of their life?

Life happens all around us. Things we do today effect what our life will be tomorrow. If you consciously attempt to do good things, if you go out of your way to say nice things and do good things for, (even to the people you don't like), then the world becomes a better place.

Like the old saying goes, *"If you break it you bought it."* If you damage the life of someone it falls on your shoulders to undo the damage and fix what you have broken.

Care enough to care. Turn off your ego, turn off your misguided sense of self and make the life of anyone you have hurt better instead of worse. If you do, not only does the life of the person you hurt become better, (and maybe they will forgive you), but your life becomes better, as well. Why? Because you have stepped outside of your ego and your unthinking mind and have done something for the greater good instead of simply doing something for yourself.

* * *

08/06/16 09:11

Does what you did yesterday define who you are today?

*   *   *

08/06/16 07:16

Today is a new day. But, can you accept it as a new day? Or, do your thoughts hold you bound to yesterday?

I Broke It. Now What?
07/06/16 09:04

I am so often confronted with the fact that people do bad things to other people and they do not care. Though this seems to be a condition of modern society, does it really have to be?

For example, somebody ran into my parked car in Venice last week. As there were a lot of people around they left a note on a napkin, *"Sorry."* They also wrote down a phone number but it was an out of service phone number. So, were they really sorry? No, they were just playing the game and protecting themselves from a charge of hit and run.

Though my insurance will fix my car, what was broken was broken and I didn't do it. Someone else did it to me and they didn't care enough to care — they didn't take responsibility for their actions and fix what they had broken. And this, I believe, is where many of the problems of the world begin and why so many people's lives go astray — they do not fix what they have broken.

I believe that everyone (meaning you) really needs to look at themselves whenever they interact with anyone. What are you creating with your interactions? Are you thinking only about yourself or are you thinking about what you are doing to the lives of others? What do your actions instigate?

People do bad things and damage the lives of other people all the time. Some of these things are done consciously while others are not. I imagine the person who ran into my car didn't mean to do so. Yet, the action was done and it was instigated on the part of that driver. Did he or she own their actions? No. Instead, they went into a state of denial and deceit. Do you believe this is the way his or her actions should have been handled? What would you have done if you hit a parked car?

Life crisis creating actions are instigated and performed by people who are so locked into their own mind that what they do they do without ever thinking about others. From this, they damage the lives of others. Once this is done, what do they do to fix what they have broken? Most do nothing. They lie, they hide, they make interpersonal excuses to themselves, and they run. But, what they have created is damage.

You have to ask yourself, *"What ultimately happens to the person who hurts another and does nothing?"* Do they ultimately succeed in life or does their lack of control, lack of consciously caring, and lack of taking responsibility for what they done eventually lead to their downfall?

What do you do? What do you do when you have entered someone's life, either by choice or by accident, and you have damaged that life? How do your fix it?

Like my car, things can be fixed. Yes, it may not ever be totally the same. But, maybe in some ways it will be better. But, nothing can ever be repaired if you don't take it to the body shop and actually try to fix it.

Most people run away from the responsibility instigated by their actions. Though they may damage the life of the young and the old, in their mind they make excuses for what they have done. This is lowest level of human consciousness; i.e., lying to yourself, making excuses for, and not caring about what you have done. When you should, in fact, be ashamed of yourself.

I can say to you that you should care. I can say to you that you should care about others as much as you care about yourself. I can say to you that you should man-up and actually take responsibility and try to fix anything that you have broken. But, it is you who must care enough to care. It is you who must stop focusing only on yourself and step outside of your selfish mindset long enough to do what it takes to fix what you have broken. It's not easy but it is what is right.

The fact is, as long as you never try to repair what you have done it will remain forever broken. What overall impact do your think that will have on your life?

Will anybody hear this and do something good for those they have wronged? I don't know. But, you must realize anything that is done and perceived as negative has a sourcepoint. There is one person who does one thing that sets it all in motion. It is the person of consciousness who then decides, if they are the sourcepoint, to fix what they have broken, undo what they have done, and make the life of those who were hurt better.

Who are you? What do you do when you break something?

All That Magic Stuff
07/06/16 07:17

Have you ever known anyone who was involved in ceremonial magic or witchcraft? I have. The thing I find interesting about these people is that they consciously study a pathway to gain control over the physical and metaphysical elements of our atmosphere and then, once they have gained this understanding, attempt to alter not only the physical landscape but the minds and the lives of people, as well. Meaning, they study spells to alter the physical environment by attempting to guide and alter the ethereal elements of the physical and mental universe and, in some cases, to take control over people's minds by making a person feel things and/or encounter things that they normally and natural would not.

For example, there are spells to make a person love someone, to make a person be sexually attracted to someone, to make someone suffer, to cause bad energies to enter a person's life, to cause good energies to enter a person's life, and the list goes on.

People that practice ceremonial magic study and preform a series of techniques that will supposedly make someone do or feel something that they would not feel or experience had that spell not been enacted.

Whether you believe in this or not is relatively unimportant in that the performer of these spells believes that they can control the mind of another individual and the energies that they will come into contact with and then they set about on a course to do just that. For those who are not avid practitioner of magic but they desire specific reactions from a person, they may go to some practitioner who promises that they can create the desired effect in another person's life.

Hand-in-hand with these spells, the person who is being spelled is not only mentally attacked but they are also often feed some hidden herb or magical something that they were not aware they were touching or ingesting. As most of these herbs or serums are not as potent as say a medical drug, they may have little physical or mental effect. Though I have known of a few cases where they caused a person to become very ill. All this to make a person feel or experience something that they were not naturally or karmiclly inclined to feel or experience.

We can look to history to see the condemnation of witchcraft. But, it is still highly and openly practiced in numerous culture across the globe. Virtually all religions are full of magical practices. Just look to the minister who prays for rain during a drought. There is, in fact, little difference between this action and those who believe that they can conjure up and alter the various elements of nature.

But, more to the point, the people that practice ceremonial magic believe that personal desire is the end-all and what a person wants they should get. But, is that valid? Think about this, somebody wants you, you don't want them, but because they employee a conjurer should you be forced to then give into their desires? And, on the other side of the issue, if someone doesn't want you, why do you think that getting them, by any means possible, is righteous and whole on any level? Furthermore, there may be the person who wants to hurt someone else for whatever reason but they are not man (or woman) enough to go face-to-face with them. Maybe they believe they will lose the confrontation be it verbal or physical but still that gives them no right to take their dislike of someone else in this other direction and, in essence, pay to have this person's life altered in some nondescript sort of way.

I believe, in life, we have all encountered people that have done something wrong to us, which made us angry, and we wanted them to hurt the way we were hurt. But, unless their damaging actions are ongoing, most of us let these occurrences go over time. Most of us as thinking, true-hearted, human beings, when we encounter situations that we don't like, people that have hurt us, or people we desire who don't desire us, we don't go to someone, have a spell cast upon that person, with the hopes that we can change their mind and make them ours or if they won't then make them suffer. We are more than that, we are bigger than that. But, you must understand that not everyone is made up of this same enlightened mindset. There are those who want revenge and/or control at all costs. But, as they cannot physically encounter a person directly, they instead turn to the back-stab of revenge magic.

But, there is a big problem in all of this. That problem is, who do these people think that they are and why do they feel they have the all-knowing understanding to make any-body do any-thing or to control any of the realms of nature?

Understandably, most people are never going to encounter a person who practices ceremonial magic and/or have a spell cast upon them. That is good. But, all of this provides you with some food for thought as there are people out there doing what you see in the movies. Yes, yes, it is not grand like on the silver screen but energy is energy and directing energy in a focused and specified manner does have the potential to affect your life, especially if someone has you encountering some foreign substance that you were not aware that you were coming into contact with.

So what does this all tell you? Let me ask, *"How superstitious are you?"* Do you believe in, *"The signs?"* Do you believe that if some specific something occurs it let's you know what is coming next? ...You know, like a black cat walking across your path... Do you believe that by doing some-thing is some specific manner some desired outcome will occur though there is no logical reason that it should? If you believe in any of the, *"Do-This,"* equals, *"That,"* sort of Magical Thinking then you have already given into the belief system that these people practice and this is what gives them control over the lives of other people.

People believe. People want to believe. People want there to be powers outside of themselves that are greater than themselves. People want to believe that there is something to turn to, to make things right when things are wrong. People want help when they call out to the cosmos for help. When help does arrive it is magical.

You give the people who practice magic all of their power. You give it to them by believing. You give it to them by you not accepting reality as reality is — by not accepting that someone people will help you, while others will hurt you — that some will like you and some will hate you.

There is no prescription for getting everything you want in life. There is no conjurer who can fulfill all of your desires. But, if you let go of desire, face life as life, then you are free and you will never need to employee a practitioner of magic.

Getting Old in the Twenty-First Century
06/06/16 12:16

When I was young and I would see older men they always had the same look: short white hair and clean shaven. If they had been a bit more suave in their younger years they may still have a mustache. They wore the same conservative dress slacks and dress shirt. Maybe a sweater if it was cold. Always hard shoes, never tennis shoes or sandals. They presented themselves with a sense of self-respect and dignity. I always respected that. That was the name of the game. Then, as opposed to now, they maintained their decorum and rarely attempted to try to look younger by projecting the style of the youthful. In fact, most hated the younger style as anybody with long hair was nothing more than a, *"Hippie."* Which were, of course, highly looked down upon back then. My father didn't even own a pair a tennis shoes and he only made it into his forties.

As for the aging women, most would dye their hair but some would not. They all wore colorful slacks and blouses with fashionable hard shoes. Most had their hair, *"Permed,"* slightly curled. My mother never even owned a pair of tennis shoes until she was in seventies when I convinced her how much more comfortable they were. She tried them on and agreed.

Back then, old was old. I felt that because I was young.

Today, when you look around all the old men also have a very generic look, as well. But, for most, it has changed. Today, pretty much every old guy you see has short white hair and a short white beard. I mean they are everywhere. Do you ever look around when you are out and about and realize how all the old guys look alike? I mean, I know several people who rock that look. If I were to be more than a few feet away from them I would not even know who they were if they called out my name — just another generic old white guy with short white hair and a short white beard.

Now, the old guy wardrobe is predominately made up of jeans and tee shirts, maybe even shorts. Gone is any sense of stature. Few ever have any advanced sense of style. If they do, they try to dress twenty years younger than their age should allow. And most, pretend to be young. But, they are not. …Don't dye your hair dudes, you're not a movie star, everybody knows what you're doing, and it just makes you look stupid.

As for aging women, they still mostly dye their hair. They too commonly wear jeans or khaki slacks. The one thing I notice about most aging women is that they cut their hair very short. You can almost chart the age of a woman by how short her hair is. The older they are, the shorter their hair. But, why is that? Why do all women of age feel that they must have short hair?

I have long discussed how it is truly a sad fact of life but so few people have any sense of personal style. And, if they once did, they lose it with the passing of time. By the time they are in their mid twenties, any sense of style is generally long gone. They have conformed to the conformity. This too has transitioned with age. Every older person looks alike and dresses alike. No one has a personal sense of style.

Where we find ourselves in history and our culture obviously dominates who we are. What we do for a living dominates who we are, how we groom our hair, and what we wear. But, within those parameters we can still be ourselves. We can still hold onto a personal sense of style and not look like everyone else.

However old you are, define your own sense of style. Be unique. Be different. Be something that is only you.

What You Search For
06/06/16 08:24

Have you ever had the experience that you have something that you want to find out about so you go to Google or Bing and you enter the topic in their search engine but you really find no answer? Then, finding nothing, you rethink the search topic and change the wording of your question but still nothing comes up so you give up your quest. Or maybe, you persist and go at it again and again: rethinking, rewording, and requestioning and, lo-and-behold, there it is, a valid and true answer to your question.

Have you ever had the experience that someone you know is searching for some answer to some question on the internet and they state, *"I can't find anything about…"* With this, you look to their search topic and you can't believe the way they worded their question; thinking, *"Of course you can't find anything by asking the question in that manner."* You reword the question for them and the answer is quickly found.

The way you quest for the answers you seek in life is really very similar to the way in which you search for something on the internet. What you find is all based upon the question(s) you ask.

The fact is, when you look for answers, though you may want to find out the truth about a certain subject, if you do not ask the right question you can never find the appropriate answer. It is also true that though you may have a certain curiousity about some subject, you may never really care enough to seek deeply enough to find a valid and true answer, so you accept the first answer you find — which may or may not be factual. And, in some cases, you already have your mind made up about the question you ask. From this, you ask all the wrong questions, guided solely by your desire to find an answer that will fulfill what you already believe.

Ultimately, the questions you ask equal the answers you will find.

How do you live your life? Do you truly seek the answers to the questions you have? Or, do you already know what you know and do not care about changing your mind even if what you believe is invalid?

Maybe you think you know the answer to questions that other people have on their mind so you put your preconceived conclusions out to the world as factual answers. This, even though, your answers are not motivated by fact but are solely defined by what you already believe.

If you put your beliefs and your preconceived answers out to the world, but you have not truly researched all the facts, all you are doing is adding to the lies that permeate the minds of the unthinking. If your answers turn out to be wrong, what does that say about you and your research? And, do you care that you have created a lie and presented it as the truth?

What you learn is defined by what you seek. What you think you know is defined by the answers to the questions that you choose to ask. What you give back from what you learn not only defines who you are but it shapes the minds of the every one.

Do you want to believe the facts or do want to believe the lies? Do you want to speak the truth or do you want to speak the lies? Your life is defined by the answers to the questions you have asked and then what you say to the world.

How hard do you question your questions? How hard do you seek the true answer to a true question?

If you seek and you cannot find, does that mean that the answer is not out there or does it mean that you have not looked long and hard enough to find the true answer to the right question?

One Minute Later
05/06/16 07:45

I was watching the new episode of the TV Series, COPS, last night. In it, there was this guy running from the police on his motorcycle. He was jamming though an intersection, against the red light, and T-Boned a guy driving his pickup truck. The guy on the motorcycle lay there breathing, but unresponsive.

Certainly, whatever happened to that guy was his fault. Don't do criminal acts and don't run from the cops. Then, you have no problem. But, if he had just driven through that interaction a minute later, the accident that happened would never have happened and the outcome to everyone's life, that was involved, would have been totally different.

Do you ever think about that, how life is lived by moments? Do you ever think about the fact that if you hadn't been in a certain place at a certain time, something very specific would not have happened to you and your life may have been totally different? This goes to both the very physical things of life, like the aforementioned motorcycle accident, onto more interpersonal things like meeting a certain person.

Myself, this ideology was forcefully brought to my attention many years ago. I was twenty-one, going to Sunday night dinner at my mother's, and bam a girl didn't see me on my motorcycle and ploughed right into me, near killing me and leaving my life forever altered. ...Happened again on my Harley when I was thirty-two, though not quite as intense. Had I left a minute earlier or a minute later my life would have been totally different.

There have been times in my life when I have encountered people where one thing lead to another; both bad and good. But, if I had not been in that place, at that moment in time, we would never have encountered one another and whatever happened between us would not have existed. I am sure that has happened to you, as well.

Do you ever think about these things? Do you question how your life would have evolved differently if you did not have a specific experience?

Though nothing ever changes the past and no experience lived can ever be undone, I think that it is important to think about and study why we have ended up where we are in life and how the choices, of when we did what, made us who we currently are. By taking the time to perform this mental exercise we can truly come to a new understanding of what leads us to this moment in time and how we can hopefully make our future moments better.

It is important to note, however, that though being in a specific place at a specific time has the potential to truly alter your life, much of your life will be orchestrated by how and what other people consciously do to you and for you.

Think about this, when you are going somewhere do you have a specific reason why you are gong there? You probably do and you probably have a desired outcome in your mind. When you meet a person or are going to interact with a specific person, do you have a specific reason why you want them in your life? Yes, you probably do. Therefore, in your mind, you are attempting to chart out what you do and why you do. And, this is the same for everyone.

This being said, what you have in mind for a specific experience may not be what someone else has in mind for that same experience — what you desire and what you want to happen may not be what they desire and what they want to happen. So, though your life's intersect in a specific moment, your individual desires for that moment may be completely different.

Let's fact facts, people do bad things. People do selfish, judgmental, violent, and things that are simply wrong. They do this, yet their mind is only focused upon themselves and the way they perceive reality. Thus, the person jamming though the intersection, running from the cops, does not really care about you or what will happen to your life due to what he (or she) does.

This is the same with people who consciously set about on a course to do something to someone else. Whether they are hoping for a positive or a negative outcome to the person they are focusing their energy upon, it is them doing something, not you asking for that something to be done. Thus, if someone does something to you seeking a predetermined outcome, it is still you who is left with the consequences of their actions. This, when you had nothing to do with instigating the situation.

Though there is, of course, karma and divine retribution attached to every action a person consciously instigates and performs, do you think most people care? No. If they do not have to immediately pay the consequences for their actions, like the aforementioned motorcycle rider, they never look back and view or care about any damage that they have done. At best, they justify and/or deny what they have done. They believe they were right and who cares about what happened to the life of the other person.

So, this is life… What you do now, in this very moment, has the potential to set the stage for the rest of your life. The choice you make, of what you do next, and the second you decide to do it, can alter everything; either for the better or for the worse. Just like the pickup truck that was run into by the fleeing motorcycle, we can never truly know what will happen next. But, with some conscious thought, we can, at least, try to never alter the life of anyone in a negative manner by thinking before we do — by looking to the future and thinking about what our actions have the potential of creating and mostly by caring about others and considering them in every action that we make before we choose to do it.

The rest of your life is defined by this moment. When are you going to decide to do what?

She's Playing a Game of Hide n' Seek That She Can Never Win
04/06/16 08:18

A couple of weeks ago I told you about the heartbreaking passing of my best bud of a cat. He was diagnosed and pretty much passed away overnight. You can read about it down below. It is still a very emotion churning experience every time we think about him. As for me, I mean he is not walking all over my desk and keyboard every time I am trying to get something done. It is a constant reminder…

We also have another cat. FYI for you cat owners… One, never let your cats live outside. It is simply too unsafe. Two, cats are not solitary creatures as some people believe. They can't be alone. If you leave them alone, they truly suffer. This, from years of personal experience.

Anyway, as our cat that passed-away never had the chance to get old and was never really sick, our other cat had no anticipation of him going away. We intellectually knew and witnessed what happened. But she, (our other cat), did not.

When he was first gone she would go to places he hung out. Finding nothing, she probably just assumed he was coming back later. Recently, she has been going on long quests, looking in the closets, behinds the couch, around the furniture, and under the bed. Then, she walks around loudly meowing, like she is saying, *"Where are you?"* I told my lady about this and she exclaims with tears in her eyes, *"She's playing a game of hide n' seek that she can never win."* Of course, as poetic as that statement was, it pops all of the emotions up front and center. *"Come out come out wherever you are."*

Some people falsely believe that animals do not have emotions. Those are people who have never been with one. They each have totally unique personalities and are completely emotionally driven creatures. If you have never become close to one (or more) I really suggest you do, they make your life so much better. You learn so much about life and yourself.

I think back to two cats we brought into our lives as kittens, many-many years ago. They loved each other. They were total soul mates. About fifteen years deep, one of them, the male, became ill. Over the next six months or so, the illness caught up with him. When he left and no longer retuned the other cat, the female, just slowly disintegrated. Her love was so strong. She died not too long after him.

You sometimes hear about these stories with people. …People who really loved each other and grew old together. One dies and the other soon follows by natural causes soon after.

Eastern spiritually often teaches that one should hide from their emotions, run away from them, stuff them down somewhere deep inside and control them; don't feel, as emotions are not good and not holy. Bullshit! Love and the positive emotions of companionship and interaction are the most inspiring and revealing emotions one can feel.

Sadly though, no one lives forever. So, if you love, you are going to lose. But, at least you did love. Love is the greatest (and most painful) emotion ever. You really should feel it.

* * *

03/06/16 16:49

Sometime you have to clean house.

* * *

03/06/16 14:28

Your life is not defined by what you do for yourself. It is defined by what you do for others.

There's One of Those Everyday
03/06/16 14:28

I have this one friend that whenever the evening is rolling around and I suggest that we go and watch the sunset she says, *"Why? There's one of those everyday."* This always just blows me away. I mean, the sunsets are all so special. They are just a perfect moment in time, each unique onto themselves. No matter where I am, I always try to take the time and witness the sunset.

…As someday, when your time is gone, you will not be able to witness *"One of those,"* everyday.

I know this one lady who photographs the sunset every day. What a great way to document history and a lifetime. I mean, each sunset is so unique onto itself that it is just pure art in the making. Every one of her photographs documents a scene and a vision that will never occur again.

My love for the sunset began many years ago. I have this very vivid memory of when I was a young adult, living in my first apartment. I had come home from my college classes. I was tired so I dozed off for what I thought would be just a couple of minutes. But, when I woke up, it was totally dark outside. It was during the winter so the days were short. But, I was so upset with myself that I had let a day go by without taking notice of its ending. I vowed to never let that happen again.

Sometimes, due to the weather, I can't actually watch the sun set. But, when I can, I always try to make the time.

As I live on the west coast, I always think about what is going on, on the other side of the world, as the sun sets on the horizon and is traveling that direction. I think of visions of Tokyo, Hong Kong, Bangkok, and India; remembering what it is like when the sun sets there.

It is really very meditative to witness the sun set.

I always love the experience when I am retuning from Asia, for I watch the sun set on the plane and then I watch the sun rise, leading into the same day as the one I had just lived — crossing the international dateline and all. It's great. You get to relive that day. I always try to make it down to the ocean on those days of return and watch the sun set again for the second time on the same day.

Very mystical, I think. Living the same day again. Maybe if a plane can go fast enough someday, they will find a method to turn back the hands of time. That would be cool.

So, for all of you who think, *"There's one of those everyday,"* you should really rethink your drink. Life is so short and the sunset is the perfect meditative way to chart the course of your history while you witness the beauty and perfection of this world that we live in.

* * *

03/06/16 07:34

Do you ever think about what you are doing before you do it?

* * *

03/06/16 07:33

You are not going to like every answer that you receive.

That Used To Be Me
02/06/16 13:32

Have you ever been out in public and you encounter someone behaving is a very unacceptable manner and you realize, *"That used to be me?"*

In life, we all evolve as human beings. Through time and experience, we gain new and deeper understandings about how to interact with people and the world.

Most of us, thought time, come to be a better version of ourselves. …Better than we were in times gone past.

This is not always the case, however. Some people actually do become worse versions of them self through time. They become more self-focused, more judgmental, more vain, and more uncaring. Some, in fact, become consciously hurtful of others. But, most of us are not like that. Though many of us experienced physiological, psychological, or experiential traumas in our life that initially made us learn the wrong way to behave, we eventually take a long hard look at ourselves, maybe find religion or become involved with psychotherapy, and gain control over how we interacted with those around us and life in general. From this, we become a better version of our self.

Some people are good throughout their life. They had good parents, grew up liked and loved, experienced no deep emotional or psychological trauma, and emerged as a good person doing only good things. Good for them!

But, most people, who act out inappropriately, are the ones who did not grow up in a loving atmosphere, did not find support from their family and friends, and were taught the wrong way to behave either through experiencing it, witnessing it, or actually being taught how to do something. These are the people who are out there, doing all that inappropriate stuff.

People who do the Right Things are generally the ones who are seen as good. People that do Bad Things are the ones who are generally seen as bad. But, in some cases, there is a fine line between what is good and what is bad.

People pursue what they desire. Though they may do this via an unobtrusive manner, none-the-less, they are going after what they want. Have you ever experienced someone who wanted you or wanted something from you but you could not give them what they wanted? Was their advancement helpful to your life? Probably not. Their pursuing what they desired set your life into chaos. Though the world may have seen them as doing nothing wrong, would you say the same thing? Probably not. Your life was invaded. It was damaged. Yet, they probably blamed you for YOU not giving THEM what THEY wanted.

There may even be people out there, that you have never met, who have the potential to bring bad things into your life. People assume they have all kinds of rights and they say or do anything that they want about you or anybody else. But, if what they are saying or doing is hurtful, is that right? Maybe their actions are not legally wrong but aren't they morally wrong? Shouldn't morality trump legality?

The fact is, sublet forms of life-invading human interactions take place all the time. Though they may be seen as benign, are they? Your life has been negatively affected, yet the person who gave you the infection can claim no wrong doing. Is that right?

In life, we are going to see those people who are behaving badly. In life, we are going encounter people that are throwing fits, committing crimes, hurting people, hurting animals, and damaging life in general. Though we probably cannot stop them, we can become more than they are. We can become the best version of our self; learn how to take control of our life, and make everyone who encounters us happy that they did so.

A better life begins by doing better things. Let that BETTER begin with you.

**Get Your Money for Nothing
Get Your Chicks for Free**
01/06/16 07:32

To quote the lyric from the Dire Straits song, *"Get you money for nothing get your chicks for free,"* as it seems an appropriate way to set this up…

It is always amusing to me (and maybe you) when I hear about some celebrity and their list of expenses. This information usually comes out when a couple is getting divorced and one of them is seeking spousal support. I mean, is simply insane the amount of money some people spend on their monthly food bill, their personal chef, their dining out, their entertainment, their clothing bill, their personal trainers, their rent, their makeup, their car upkeep, their travel, and all their etc.… This, when most of us struggle to get by.

I think each of us has an idea of what we would do with the money, if we had that much of it. Some people would use it buy every dream they ever had. Some would buy things for their family and their friends. But, that is all fantasy. Here are people that actually have it and what do they do with it? Do they live a humble life and use their financial success to help those in need? No, instead they live a lavish lifestyle and feel that they deserve to continue to do so. I don't know, I just don't get it???

I think this points to the vanity of modern humanity. They haves, have. How they got it does not matter. Yet, once they have it they can do anything they want with it but the one thing they never seem to do is to think about anyone else but themselves.

Now, certainly not everyone who gains financial success is like this. But, I would venture to say that most are. They do whatever it takes to get to where they want to be and then all they do is focus on themselves, their lifestyle, and what they want. But, what do they want? I believe that the eventually collapse of so many of the lives and the lifestyles of those with large amounts of money goes to the source of the problem. I mean how many of these once very successful people fall into drug or alcohol abuse and end up in bankruptcy? A lot... Yet, do they look to the source of their problem? Does anyone? They just get money and spend it on themselves.

Do you, as a person, spend any time giving back to people, society, the needy, the whomever? Do you ever consciously reach out your hand to help those in need? Or, do you simply focus on yourself?

From my experience, very few of the people whom I have met throughout my lifetime have spent any of their time actually thinking about others to the degree that they actually go out and try to help. Instead, they only think about what they want and set about on a course to obtain it.

Money is not the only way to give back and to help. In fact, many people with loads of money give some of it away to the so-called charities in order to lower their taxes. Though this may help the greater good in some small way, giving is only giving when you actually give of yourself, just as caring is only caring when you actually care. Giving money to get a tax break is not giving. That is taking.

People with little money can sit at their computer or talk on their phone and waste their life helping no one while desiring everything. Just as people with lots of money can waste their life by eating at the best restaurants or having their personal chefs prepare only the best food just the way they like it. Or both, the less than affluent and the rich could get up off of their butts, stop thinking only about themselves, and actual get out there and do something that makes a positive difference to the people who actually need a helping hand.

Certainly, in our society, the rich and the famous our revered. But, why is that? What have they actually done? Yes, they have become rich and famous, but what have the done for the betterment of the world in their process of become rich and famous? What have you done? If you personally cannot answer that question about yourself, you really should take a long, hard look at the way you are living your life and think about what you are actually doing with your life, how you will be remembered, and what will you have to show for your existence here on earth. In other words, stop being selfish, stop only thinking about yourself, get up off of your butt, and actually get out there and help somebody!

* * *

01/06/16 07:18

Speculation is the biggest cause of individual life destruction and world chaos that anyone can unleash.

This is Time
31/05/16 14:08

As anyone who reads this blog or knows anything about me understands, I've written a lot about comprehending and coming to terms with the concept of time. Certainly, the Master Text on the subject is my book, *Zen O'clock: Time to Be*. I wrote that book in the mid 1980s. It was first published, by an independent publisher, in the late 80s with the title, *"Time,"* and later by a major publisher in '97. Since then it has been translated into a bunch of languages and distributed around the world. Donald G. Jackson, my Zen Filmmaking brother, liked the Intro. to that book so much that he read it as the invocation for the faux-wedding in *The Roller Blade Seven*. All this being said, I believe that one of the essential questions to life, that each person must frequent ask themselves is, *"How am I experiencing and dealing with the passing of time?"*

For each of us, there is a prescribed amount of time that we will be here in our physical bodies. Many people hold onto the hope and the belief that there is some forever out there, where we will be the best incarnation of ourselves and our souls will live on forever. Maybe… But, nothing is guaranteed. As such, what we live here and now, in these ever-aging bodies, is all we have to hold onto. We, as living human beings, are elementally defined by the passing of time.

When we are young there is the undefined belief that we have forever. Many of us never think about the passing of time. We do what we do when we do it and time just passes on. For most people there comes a moment of realization when they conclude, time has passed, they are getting older, they do not have forever, and, as such, they must truly focus upon what they are doing with their time and how they are living their life. Some, however, though they may be brought to this realization through personal reflection or via the dying of someone close to them, never truly takes this concept to heart and they simply pass through their life defined only by whatever desire, emotion, or life-event they are experiencing in any given moment.

In life, throughout all countries and cultures, few people have the time to take the time to think about time. Their life-time is dominated by doing their job, whatever that job may be, in order to pay the bills to live, eat, and raise their family. They pass through life understanding that they should take some time but that time is never allotted to them. Or, perhaps better put, they never take the time to make the time. They allow life, and the responsibilities thereof, to control their entire existence.

There is the other side of the coin, as well. Some people have the time to contemplate time. Maybe they were born wealthy, maybe they received an inheritance, or maybe they personally made a lot of money that allowed them to retire at an early age. But, people in this situation are rarely any different than the average Joe. They rarely take the time to look at their time.

To understand time, you have to make the time to understand time. How do you do this? You stop the doing.

Most people never sit in silence. They never step beyond the doing. They have their desires which they pursue, they have their bills to pay, they have their friends and their family that they do what they do with them, but they never take the time to sit back and be silence in order to come to an understanding of life's realities of which time is one of the biggest. When they have a vacation they never STOP, they just DO. They go, and even if what they do causes them to relax, they never take the time to stop their thinking mind and come to terms with time.

In other writings, I have spelled out methods that may help one come to terms with understanding time. What I often witness from the communications I receive from people who have read those writings is, however, that people intellectualize them. They look to them as a method to gain a handle on time. But, the fact is, there is no method to control time. I can give you pointers to understand time but you have to be able to let go of what you want from time in order to grow an awareness of time.

Right now, if you are reading this, you have the time to study time. STOP! LET GO! This is your time. I really mean it, STOP!

Stop your mind from racing. Stop your mind from thinking whatever your mind is thinking about. Stop it and just be.

What do you hear? What do you see? What does you body feel like? This is your time. This is who you are in this time.

This time; this moment, is all that there is, stop thinking about anything else because it may never happen. This moment is all you have; feel it.

Now, take a look at what this time feels like. What is it? What is this moment to you? What does this moment mean? How does this moment feel?

How are you encountering and moving though this moment? How will what you are doing, in this moment, affect your next moment? Is what you are thinking, feeling, and doing in this moment allowing your next moment to be better or is it setting karma into motion?

How you feel here, is how you feel here. What you do here, is what you do here. How you feel here and what you do here affect your next forever for everything you do in any given moment creates what you will next encounter in the next moment, the next hour, the next day, the next year. What are you creating in this moment that will set the stage for the rest of your time?

To understand time, you must embrace time. To comprehend time, you must STOP and study time. To thrive in your time, you must become one with time.

Tick tock, this is your time. How are you embracing it and how are you encountering it?

This is your time. It is for you to decide how you live your time. But, if you do not embrace the pure essence of time, blame no one but yourself when your time is gone.

*　　*　　*

31/05/16 07:37

"It happened for a reason."

Who decides what that reason is?

Behind the Wheel and the Actions of Others
30/05/16 15:26

I forever find that the interaction you have with other drivers while you are behind the wheel is very telling about a person's personality — how they encounter life and the wake that they leave behind themselves to all those that they encounter. There are the angry drivers, the brain dead drivers, the distracted drivers, there are the speed demons, and the too old to be behind the wheel in the first place drivers… The list goes on but these are a few of the frequently encountered driving types.

How a person drives demonstrates how they interact with life. You can learn a lot about a person by the way they drive. Many times more than you want to know…

I was driving today and I attempted to turn into a driveway that has an opening only large enough for one car to pass through. This driveway is on the downward slope of a hill and the cars generally travel quite fast as they drive down this hill. So, you have to be very careful as you turn into this driveway.

In any case, I put on my turn signal, slowed down, and begin to turn in. There, right at the opening of the driveway, hiding behind the wall, was an old white lady in her white economy class car completely blocking my progression forward. What she was doing there, I don't know? She was doing some nondescript something. But, what she wasn't doing was thinking about anybody but herself.

As stated, I attempted to pull in. Instead of seeing an oncoming car and understanding the situation of the fast passed hill and backing up to let me in, she looked at me, put her car in drive and moved forward. This, when she had an entire parking lot behind her. She could have easily backed up.

Me, I honked at her to let her know this was an inappropriate action on her part and I pointed so that she could understand that she should back up. Nothing... She kept her forward progression. She did not care at all about me or the situation she was creating.

This being the case and to keep her from hitting me, all I could do was to back up onto the street, which caused a car racing down the hill to slam on his brakes and come to a screeching halt — close to hitting me. But, she didn't care. I honked, told her to back the fuck up, but nothing, she kept moving forward. The guy behind me was yelling. But she, not thinking about anybody but herself, just slowly squeezed her way out of the driveway and drove on.

Some people think about others. In fact, some people think about others first. This is a good thing. They are usually the good drivers and the nice people. A lot of people think of no one but themselves. They do not care about what is going on, what they are instigating, and/or what they have created. All they do is what they do when they want to do it.

Who are you? How do you encounter life? How do the people you associate with encounter life? How do you drive and how do they drive?

How you drive says a lot about how you encounter life and what you will create in life.

* * *

30/05/16 14:40

Just because a person appears to have everything doesn't mean that they actually do.

* * *

30/05/16 14:14

Do you want to belong or do you want to think for your self?

* * *

30/05/16 14:14

Just because you write a script does not mean that the movie is going to be made.

All of These People Doing All of These Things
30/05/16 08:28

Have you ever had the opportunity to look down at a city from atop a tall building? What you will see is that there are a million people doing a million things. There are cars driving, people walking, and trucks driving by full of something. Each and every one of these people has a believed purpose in doing what they are doing. They each have all of the thoughts, emotions, and desires that we all possess. They each are an enclosed entity onto themselves. There is all this going on around you and yet, there you are, believe that you are the only one that matters — locked up into feeling whatever it is you are feeling.

There has been New Age philosophy going around forever that we are all, *"One."* But, do you feel like, *"One?"* Do you feel that you are part of that person in the back of your mind that you don't like? Do you feel at one with that bum you see sitting there on the street corner, in dirty clothing, drunk and begging for money? Do you feel at one with the person who is so rich that they can buy and do anything that they want? Do you feel at one with that person who hurt you?

To pass your consciousness off to the nonsense of mind games philosophy does a disservice to you, the person. But, to be so selfish to believe that what you are feeling is any more valid and important that what anyone else is feeling does a disservice to humanity. Simply open up your eyes to the world around you and you will see that you are, at best, a cog in this vast wheel of life.

People who live in an isolated setting believe themselves to be the center of the universe. This isolation can be physical but, in this modern world, it is more than likely psychological.

There are those who move among us who appear to interact in a normal way. They speak with others, they buy their groceries, they have a job, they may even go to church on Sunday. But, what they do not possess is the mental maturity and intelligence to understand that what they are doing, what they are thinking, and what they are feeling is not the sourcepoint for the way all of this world should feel — what they believe is not how all of the world should believe. From this, they try to cast their beliefs, based upon isolationism, out to the world around them. They may do this in small ways; by behaving in an inappropriate manner and attempting to make those around them experience any emotional dissatisfaction and/or personal pain just as they are feeling it. Or, they may do this in a big way. They may do things that are so horrendous that they impact the lives of many people in a negative manner. In either case, what they do is based upon them disregarding others and experiencing life defined solely by what they think, feel, or by believing all should believe just as they believe.

Do you allow what you feel to control how you behave? Do you allow it to control you even if you understand that what you feel and what you do, based upon those feelings, may hurt someone else?

Do you believe that what you say and what you do should be embraced by all the people who come into contact with you? Do you ever take the time to think that perhaps you are wrong? …That there is another way to look at the situation? And then, do you make excuses and justifications, in your own mind, for taking the actions you have taken based upon your feelings and understandings? If you do then you are operating your life based upon a very selfish perspective.

Selfishness only leads to the deteriorating Self.

If you take the time to stand atop a tall building and look down to all the goings-on down below you, if you take the time to step outside of your own selfishness and limited persona driven definition of life, you may have the opportunity to witness that you are not the only one that matters. From this, you may stop being a self-driven, selfish person. And, from this realization you may actually be able to care more about someone else than you care about yourself. You may actually make the world just a little bit better instead of allowing it to continue its selfish, self-driven experiment in the destruction of others based upon isolated, self-driven thoughts.

* * *

29/05/16 20:15

You are not an expert on anyone else's life but your own.

What gives you the right to pass judgment on them?

*   *   *

29/05/16 20:12

You can't undo what you can't undo.

But, if you don't try that means that you don't care.

Caring or not caring is what provides the definition of your life.

*   *   *

29/05/16 20:11

Do you think about other people before you do what you do?

If you don't that says a lot about you.

The Mysteries of the Universe
28/05/16 08:04

I recently heard this one very well-known spiritual soothsayer suggesting a few sources that he thought would feed the minds of those seeking information about the mysteries of the universe. I popped over to them and it almost made me laugh. It was simply a different guy saying the same things… …The things we have all heard before. *"Let go of the thoughts in your mind. Breathe in and breathe out… Feel the essence of the universe entering your being."*

The reason it almost made me laugh is ask yourself, *"Do you care about that kind of thing?"* Most people don't. What most people care about is living life the way the want to live it, having money, having friends, having possessions, having sex, having power, eating good food, and doing good things.

Most people are angry at life. They are angry because they do not have all of the things that they want and the world does not operation in a fashion that they desire. They may not express this fact. They may hide this fact to other people. But, angry is what they are. They are angry at everything from the way they look, to the way they feel, to what they don't have, onto what someone else said or did. They don't care about making themselves better. They don't want to consciously breathe. They just want a new reason to fuel their anger.

Yes, there are some people out there who do seek out a deeper knowledge. But, these people are few and far between. And, like I often declare, the problem with people who follow this path is that they place themselves, and those who teach this path, on a pedestaled; believing that they are somehow better and more enlightened than those who are not on this path.

So, what are we left with? Two things… One, people who are angry at the world. Two, people who either try to make money or make themselves look MORE than <u>the others</u> by claiming to understand the path of consciousness. Equaling the fact that those on the path of consciousness, teaching the supposed mysteries of the universe, are all basing their life upon falsehoods.

The fact is, you can discuss the subtle realms of reality until you are blue in the face. You can claim inner-peace and inner-knowledge and set about on a path to actualize and teach it. You can do all of this until you have nothing to eat or your life is invaded by some stranger doing something you do not like, then it all changes. You may claim peace on the inside but on the outside you have to get down to it and find to a way to keep yourself alive.

The mysteries of the universe can only be contemplated when you have a paycheck, or are riding high on someone else's money, and have a full belly. That is the ultimate truth to those who want to understand the mysteries of universe.

The Screenplay of Life
27/05/16 08:43

Have you ever been watching a TV show or a movie and your mind becomes agitated thinking about how, if that was you living that moment, you would have done things totally differently? Have you ever been watching a TV show or a movie and you begin to think about how you can't understand why the characters did the things that they did? Have you ever watched a TV show or a movie and later found your mind wandering to the fact of the character development in that show and how it was impossible for you to believe that they did what they did in the way they did it and how you would have done it totally differently? You know it was simply a theatrically presentation but, none-the-less, you find yourself thinking about the outcome.

Life is very much like the screenplay of a film. It is all lived out there. There are all of these things going on that you have no control over. People do not do what you think they should do. People do not behave in the way you want them to behave. People do not act the way you think they should act. The outcome of the various life situations do not play out in the way you would like them to play out. And, all of this stuff goes on and you have absolutely no control over it.

Most of us, when we encounter life situations that we do not like, obviously think about and re-think the situation. That is simply part of the human condition. What occurred may make us angry, it may make us frustrated, it may even make us sad. But, the one thing it does do, for sure, is it makes us feel. It makes us feel the way we do not want to feel. From this, we begin to think about the people and the things that we have no control over. Some play the scenario over-and-over again in their mind, obsessing about the person and the outcome. Some become so obsessed with the person and the thoughts of and about the situation that they improperly feel that they have the right to invade the life of the person or person's who were involved and do all kinds of inappropriate things.

Think about this, have you ever done something that someone didn't like and from that they went to all kinds of lengths to say, do, or actually act out things that really hurt your life?

Think about this, have you ever been upset with someone and what they did and how it affected you that you went out of your way to damage their life?

There are all kinds of things people do in these situations but they are all based upon one premise, they did not like the outcome of the screenplay of life. In other words, they made a choice not to like a person or a situation and set on a course of obsessing about that person and situation and then begin to act out in a pattern that they hoped would negatively affect that person by broadcasting their dissatisfaction to the world.

For those of you who read this, many of you will undoubtedly think about a life event that you lived through and did not like. You will realize that though it may have upset you at the time, you worked through it, and eventually let it go without attempting to do any damage to the people involved in the event. This is the conscious, adult way to handle these life events. But, a lot of people are not functioning adults nor are they thinking, caring, and/or conscious. They are locked in a life space of unenlightened unfulfillment and they do all that they can do to bring down the life of any person to their level. They feel something, so should you. They try to either rewrite the script of life or they try to add the next scene to the script of life. But, by doing this, all they do is to add to the negative melodrama of life.

Think about this, has an event ever happened in your life that you did not like. Once that even happened did you feel what you felt and then set about on a course to bring attention to that event? What was the outcome? Did it make you feel better? Did it make the other person feel worse? Did it actually help you and did it actually damage them? In either of these cases, did it undo what was done — which would be the only thing that would truly make you feel better or did it simply set a new scene of the melodrama of life into motion?

The fact is, if you live a life moment and then you extend the screenplay of that moment by acting upon your emotions the only true outcome is that you make yourself look worse, you make yourself look like the victim, you make yourself look weak, you make yourself look like you are not strong enough to actually deal with the realities of life.

In life, you are not going to like the outcome of every movie you watch. You are going to think that the characters should have done something differently. You are going think that you could have written a better script. But, this is life, everyone writes their own screenplay and you have no control over the outcome. If you can accept this, you pass though life understanding life while not trying to control life. From this, though you may not like all of the life events you encounter at least people will see you as strong and in charge instead of weak and dominated by the actions of others.

Regenerating Neighborhoods
AKA Destroying Historic Culture
26/05/16 14:19

I went to see an exhibit at the *Hauser Wirth & Schimmel Gallery* yesterday. I find it curiously interesting whenever I go to an exhibit and I like the ambiance of the gallery more than the instillation. I mean, *Hauser Wirth & Schimmel* is housed in this beautiful repurposed conglomerate of buildings. The designers did an incredible job of keeping the vintage bricked-laid essence of the facility while bringing it up to code for the twenty-first century.

Though the gallery is awesome, the neighborhood; well...

Let me go into a little bit of history on the vicinity for those of you who may not know. This area of L.A. is now known as, *The Art's District.* It is just a bit East of *Little Tokyo* and a bit North East of *Skid Row.* Back in the late 70s there was a great junkyard bar, located there, that became a punk rock haven, *Al's Bar.* Long gone... By the 80s the area became known as, *The Loft District,* as it was one of the first places in L.A. that artists and musicians congregated as they were able to find a place to live and work in these old industrial buildings where rent was cheap and the undefined space was vast. The area was dangerous but the cool, the hip, and the artsy did move in. Though I never considered myself any one of the three, I too had a space down there.

The thing that I loved about this area is that it was made up of beautiful, failing architecture. There were just the most aesthetically pleasing walls covered in graffiti, dirt covered alleys, and buildings slowly falling into rubble. I loved it! As I became a filmmaker, I cannot tell you how many scenes in how many movies I filmed within a few block radius of *Hauser Wirth & Schimmel.*

Anyway, after we saw what there was to see in the gallery, we took a walk around the neighbor. Though I quite frequently hang out in nearby *Little Tokyo* and DTLA, it had been a couple of years since I actually took a walk around, *The Art's District*.

It is really sad. All the places I used to film are now redesigned and repurposed, made to look like horrible interpretations of modern buildings. I have been watching this as the years have gone on but to walk the streets and see the rejuvenation was really sad. No more abandon buildings that yeah, you either had to go into strapped or with a group of people if you hoped to film and walk about unscathed. But, that was all part of the fun. No more dirty, polluted, trash ridden alleys. No more abandoned railroad tracks covered in years of old weeds and the occasional dead junky. No more graffiti. Only old buildings made to look new, protected by security guards.

You know… With everything new, everything revamped, reenvisioned, reestablished, regenerated, and all of those other res… you really lose something that was beautiful. Something that you will never see again.

…Never seen again unless you watch a Zen Film. But, nobody does that so never mind. ☺

* * *

24/05/16 15:06

This day is passing. What do you have to show for it?

Escaping the Cults
24/05/16 14:53

Throughout these modern days of history there has been so much press given to, *"Cults."* Basically, a cult is anything that draws people into the fray, generally with some sort of religious ideology at its basis. But, the ideology of a cult is much bigger than that. And, in fact, it is much smaller. In reality, a cult is simply some entity that exists beyond the acceptance of the commonly held belief system that holds a person bound to where they are, whether they want to be there or not.

...Let's not forget, in a lot of cultures Christianity is considered a cult.

Growing up when I did, and my mind being focused on the realms of consciousness that it was, I encountered a lot of people and/or groups that could be (and, in fact, were) considered cults. To me, they were just new forms of thinking. But, to the masses they were seen as something much more devious.

I remember my friend Steve and I used to hang out on Hollywood Blvd. a lot when we were like twelve and thirteen. The star-lined part of Hollywood Blvd... We would go and see movies, walk through the head shops, and stuff like that. All of the, *"Cults,"* would be there too, hocking their wares. *The Hare Krishnas,* the Jesus Freaks, and the like... At one point this one group, lead by this Korean guy, Sun Myung Moon, was all over the boulevard. They were inviting people to their encampment. The deal was they would pick people up in a bus at about four in the afternoon and promised to have you back by midnight. Me, I was all set to go the next weekend. In the one act of, *"You can't do it,"* discipline I ever remember receiving from my mother, she wouldn't let me go. Probably a good thing. I mean what kind of group wants thirteen-year-old boys as their disciples?

Anyway... As my year's progresses, I obviously

became involved with various eastern spiritual teachings. Some called them cults. I remember when my teacher Swami Satchidananda was asked, *"Did he brainwash people,"* he would reply, *"Why does your brain need washing?"*

In all the time I was with him, the only money I ever spent was a $10.00 donation that I choose to give when he needed a new blanket at the *L.A. Integral Yoga Institute*. Sure, I gave him thousands of hours of my time, especially as his west coast soundman, but I was replayed a thousand fold with knowledge. I mean hell… I taught the martial arts for years-upon-years for my one instructor without ever receiving a penny. Was he a cult leader? No, just a Korean martial arts teacher. And, anyone who has ever trained under a Korean teacher long enough to reach instructor level will pretty much tell you the same story — the master gives you the run of the studio but you don't make a dime.

Anyway, back to the story at hand…

As I grew older, into my mid teens, spirituality was pretty much my everything. There was this one teacher Stephen Gaskin, known to my generation simply as, Stephen. He was a spiritual teacher from San Francisco who had moved his troupe lock, stock, and barrel to a farm in Tennessee. For a time, he toured the country giving lectures. When I was about sixteen, and ready to throw away the material world, he was in town and I went up to him after one of his lectures and asked him, if I were to move to, "The Farm," (as it was known), would I have to give him my car. As it turns out, I would.

Now, here is the catch and the point and purpose of this discourse — when you join a group, religious or otherwise, cult or otherwise, if you have to give them everything how do you ever get out? For example, if I had moved to Tennessee, lived there for a time, decided I no longer liked it, how would I have been able to leave if I had donated my car to the greater whole?

And, this is the thing, and why so many people are trapped where they are trapped. ...Whether it is a cult, a religious group, a bad relationship, a bad job, or even being homeless; how do you ever get out if you have no way out? This is why the so-called, *"Cults,"* have such a hold on people. This is why the partner in a bad relationship has such a hold on their spouse. This is how the horrible boss at a terrible job keeps his employees. This is why people who are homeless have no way off of the street. If you don't have a family member or something like that who will reach out a hand to you and help you get back on your feet, you are screwed.

Religion promises you all of the promises. People promise you the love you have always dreamt of having — like the kind you see in all of the *Chick Flick,* Romance Movies. The world temps you with having it all so you spend it all trying to be seen as someone who has, *"Achieved."* All of these things can leave you broke, busted, homeless, and/or with no where to turn.

Therefore, before you ever do anything: before you ever get involved with a group that promises you inner-knowledge, before you ever fall head-over-heels for the bad boy or the bad girl, before you ever believe the lie that you can financially have it all, rethink your drink. Step back, look at your now — where you are. Step back, look at where the road you may walk down has the potential to lead you. Mostly, never believe the lies. Do what you do, believe what you believe, love who you love, but never leave yourself with no way out!

You want to escape the cult? That is the way to do it. Never give the cult absolute control over you.

The Power to Do Good
23/05/16 15:27

How do you spend your days?

We each have a limited number of days here in this life. The younger you are the less this fact is on your mind. But, the facts are the facts. Our days of life our limited.

Again, how do you spend your days? What do you do with your time? Do you help people? Do you help animals? Do you help the environment? Or, do you only help yourself?

What do you say? What do you write? Do your words help or do they hurt?

What do you think? What do you do based upon what you think? Do your thoughts lead to positive actions and deeds or do your thoughts lead to judgments and negativity?

What spreads from your thoughts, words, and actions? Do people do good things or are they instigated to be negative, judgmental, and hurtful?

You have the power to do good. The power is in you at any moment of your life. No matter what you are thinking, no matter what you are feeling, no matter what you are saying, no matter what you are doing or what is being done to you, you can choose to be the power of good.

What do you choose?

The Process, The Product, and How You Get from Here to There
23/05/16 07:43

When you wake up in the morning do you make your bed? If you do make your bed, do you put the sheets and the blankets precisely back into place or do you just rapidly pull them? When you are staying in a hotel do you make your bed at all? Or, do you simply expect that someone is going to do it for you?

When you make your morning coffee do your consciously grind your beans and then precisely put the ground beans into the coffee maker or do you just open the tub full of pre-ground coffee, scoop the desired amount into the coffee pot and let it brew to give you your AM jolt?

Have you ever watched a master chef cutting vegetables for the meal he (or she) is concocting? It is pure poetry. It is like precision magic? How do you cut vegetables when you are making your meal?

I was watching a television show last night and these hunters were justifying why they kill. They spoke about how we humans are at the top of the food chain, the only thinking animal, and how they as hunters love the land and the animals just as much as the environmentalists as they are providing a service when they kill. It went on and on... Have you ever gone out with a hunter and watched them kill? Did you witness their demeanor? Do you kill?

A hunter describing how they kill is not the same as a surfer describing why they surf. Loving something never involves killing it.

How we personally choose to interact with our life defines not only our own personal existence but this behavior expands to define the world around us. What you do, how you do it, affects you. It also affects all those who encounter your actions and witness your behavior. What you do and how you do it never only affects you.

You can live your life consciously, doing what you do with caring, refinement, and consciousness. Or, you can randomly pass through your existence reacting, overreacting, justifying your actions, and destroying all in your wake.

Living consciously is a choice. Living with a focused intent, while precisely doing the things that you are doing, is a choice. Living unconsciously involves no choice. It is simply an exhibition of random, thoughtless movement passing from birth to death.

People can find a justification for doing anything that they do. They can even make people believe what they say. But, if you have to justify your actions, you are doing something wrong. Doing something with conscious intent involves no rationalization or justification it is simply seen as perfection in action.

Who are you and why? What do you choose to do and why do you choose to do it? Finally, how do you do it? These are essential questions to have an answer for as you pass through your life.

Opinion Verses Fact and the Diction of Fiction
22/05/16 07:43

How much of your life to you spend living in fact verses how much of your life to you spend living in opinion? Is what you think about based upon facts or is what you think about based upon opinion? Do you know and/or do you care which is which?

Most people spend their entire lifetime never truly delving into the real. They simply allow themselves to pass from birth to death focusing upon their momentary moment, their momentary desire — what they want in that moment, guided only by the anger, happiness, desire, or lust they are felling in any given moment.

Right here, right now what is the focus of your life? What do you want and what are you receiving? Is what you are feeling based upon the essence of reality or is what you are feeling based upon something someone said that made you decide to feel a certain way and desire a certain thing?

People talk all the time. In the age of the internet, some people write all the time. What do they say and what do they write? When you listen to someone do you take the time to actually analyze what they speak and what they write? Or, do you simply believe it as fact, no matter what they are speaking and writing?

Just because someone says something does not make it the truth. Just as simply because someone is calling someone else a liar does not make them a liar.

What is the truth? The truth is something based upon fact and that can be proven. What is an opinion? An opinion is something someone feels. Though they may believe it to be truth, that does not make it the truth. Why? Because they did not do the research. They did not go to the source of that knowledge, they simply based what the think upon what they feel or what others have said.

Religion is based upon opinion. Faith is an opinion. Faith is opinion based upon the belief that someone or something is in control and has constructed a divine game plan.

Politics is based upon opinion. Politics is opinion based upon the hope that someone can provide you with a better, more fulfilled life and lifestyle.

Philosophy is based upon opinion. Philosophy is opinion based upon a personally constructed set of standards that are believed to present people with a better way to think and interact with life.

And the list goes on... But, these three previous described possibly life defining factions are large scale opinions. Most people never even take the time to delved deeply into them. They may go to religious services on the Sabbath, they may get all fired up about their political beliefs and become angry at the beliefs of others, thinking that they are wrong, they may even believe what they believe but at their personal core there is no focalized source point of defined knowledge. All that exists is the momentary belief in a momentary something that is actually nothing for all it does is to cause the person to feel a certain way in whatever moment they find themselves.

Who are you? Do you ever take the time to care enough to care to know what absolute true knowledge is or do you simply allow yourself to be guided through life by random emotions instigated by who know what or who knows who?

You can live your life based upon the nothingness of random emotions if you want to. You can cast your opinions out there for others to hear. But, in either case, all you are doing is setting further random chaos into motion. By doing that, not only do you hurt yourself but you damage the entire world for from this behavior nothing is based upon fact it is only based upon the fiction of your diction.

My suggestion, define a clear line between life facts and life opinions. Know the difference. And then, based your life upon facts not upon opinions.

* * *

21/05/16 07:24

Just because someone makes a statement that looks like an established fact does not make it an established fact. It is simply that person applying opinionated opinions to their personal opinion.

* * *

21/05/16 07:15

People justify their actions all the time. They find reasons for doing what they do.

Here is a simply formula to know if what you are doing is right or wrong. Have you taken something from someone else in the process of you doing what you do? If the you take that hurts someone. Thus, if you are non-consensually taking, what you are doing is universally wrong.

* * *

21/05/16 07:13

All good things are created by one person deciding to do one good thing.

All bad things are created by one person deciding to do one bad thing.

Life is created by instigation.

* * *

21/05/16 07:11

The people that have have messed with your life are always in the forefront of your memories.

* * *

20/05/16 07:37

If you live by your own set of rules what happened when you break those rules?

*   *   *

20/05/16 07:37

At what point is it too late to change?

* * *

20/05/16 07:35

Is defending a friend who has done something wrong good or bad?

Everybody Talks About the Films but Nobody Studies the Films
20/05/16 07:26

I forever find it curious that whenever I hear or read about what people are saying about the Zen Films of Scott Shaw they are virtually always completely wrong. Some have gone to extended lengths to describe and discuss the films I have made but they are completely missing the point. Some love them, some hate them, and, all that is fine with me — that is their opinion. But, no one ever studies the films.

From a personal perspective, I can tell you that from the time I was young I would watch films very carefully. I would notice things about them that I would later realize were completely missed by others. There are mistakes in continuity, changes in lighting between the various takes, wardrobe differences, actors looking at the camera, and the list goes on. But, I never saw those as filmmaking flaws, I simply saw them as part and parcel of the filmmaking process. By observing a film in this manner, it truly makes the watching of that movie very intriguing to me.

Again, from a personal perspective, I can categorically state that I have never attempted to make a traditional film. From my experience, a traditional film, that will play well to a traditional film going audience, costs a lot of money as you have to play to their preconceived notions about what a film is supposed to be. As I have never had a high budget in my filmmaking endeavors, I have never attempted to walk down that road — though some of the people I have worked with have attempted to guide me in a more traditional direction in my filmmaking practices. But, that is just not who I am.

All this being stated, what I can say is that within the spontaneity, freedom, and magic of Zen Filmmaking every film that I have ever created has been done so with a very clear focus of message, (based upon budgetary constraints, of course). You may love what I do. You may hate what I do. You may issue praise or cast criticism. That's all fine with me. But, what most people never seems to do is to actually study the films I make. They never look for the subtleties. They simply look to the obvious. And, by viewing my Zen Films in this manner, they are really missing the whole point.

...I mean, come on! These are Zen Films, what do you expect to see when you sit down to watch them?

As the filmmaker, I could point to each element of what one should be looking for in each scene of my films. But, what would be the fun of that? This is Zen Filmmaking and that is all part of the process; finding the hidden meaning, revealing to yourself what is hiding beneath the surface and what it means to you. It is essential to know, however, that every scene in every one of my Zen Films has a Some Thing that is there for a reason which guides the overall vision of the film and projects an ideology to the audience whether they consciously notice it or not. This is why they are each titled a, *"Zen Film."*

So, I want to call out all you, (oh so knowledgeable), film reviewers. I want to tell you, *"You missed the point."* Simply by looking to the storyline, the sets, the acting, and the character development for guidance in your reviews you have completely overlooked what is actually going on.

As a Film Watcher and as a Film Maker I can say that to truly understand any film you have to look beyond the obvious. This is especially the case with Zen Films. So, the next time you want to find something to cast your judgment upon at least have the foresight to see what you are missing by studying the subtitles instead of simply sitting there with your mind already made up and casting judgment.

* * *

19/05/16 09:35

If you spend your life looking for demons, you will find them.

You Are What You Speak

We have all heard the old adage, *"You are what you eat."* As truthful as that statement may be, what is even more definitive of a person's life is, *"You are what you speak."*

Think about this, how do you talk to other people and how do you speak about other people? What is your demeanor? Each person has one. Developed in childhood, it moves forward throughout one's life. Based upon personality, each person speaks with a distinct style and focuses upon specific things. Some people are loud and rude, always trying to overpower the conversation, others are soft-spoken and reserved. Some speak about what they have learned. Others speak about themselves. Some people simply tells lies at every opportunity, altering truths to suit their own needs.

Studying how other people speak and what they talk about is an essential method to come to understand the motivating factors for human consciousness. You can really learn a lot by actually taking the time to watch, listen, and study what a person is saying, how they are saying it, and then come to the conclusion of why.

It is also essential that you study how you speak; what you say and why. Most people simply pass through their life never truly taking note of how they are perceived by the rest of the world. Some don't care but all should. For it is how we are seen by the world that sets forth our opportunities.

Take a moment right now and review the people you know. Isolate them one-by-one and define how they each speak, what they each commonly speak about, how they present their message, and what occurs to their life and the lives of those around by how they present that message.

Once you have defined, in your own mind, the factors that make several of the people you know who they are, turn the microscope around on yourself. Think about your words, what you say, how you sound, what you emphasize, and the truths and/or the lies that you tell. Do you manipulate with your words or are your words based in caring about others?

Though many of us will immediately have a reason based in logic, at least in our own mind, as to why we speak the way we speak and why we say what we say, spread your analysis out farther and think about what effect you are having on those around you by speaking the way you speak; about the subjects you speak. And, perhaps most importantly, what effect do those words have on your own life? Have they helped you? Have they helped others? Or, have your words caused hurt and isolation?

Few people ever take the time to think about anything. They rarely take the time to study their why and their wherefore. The problem is, if you don't your world just becomes a mishmash of random events. Good things may happen or bad things may happen but the most essential element in that equation is you and how you interact with the world. As much of this interaction is based upon what you say to others in this world, thus, what you say and how you say it is one of the most essential elements in the evolution of your life.

Know who you are. Know what you say and why. And, then take control of what you say and how you say it. From this, not only will your own life be lived from a more conscious state of mind but your interactions with the world will be much more beneficial to the all.

Who Makes This Stuff Up?
18/05/16 08:12

For each person they have a belief in the concept of a great power, (god if you will), what happens to a person after they die, if you can or cannot communicate with angels or demons from the other side, and a million other things that tie this human form to the concept of and the desire for something more once one passes away. The concept of heaven, hell, purgatory, or reincarnation permeate the mindset of all people across the globe. This is especially the case as one grows closer to the end of their life; then the thoughts of these things become all-encompassing. But, where do all these thoughts come from? Who makes this stuff up?

Religious pundits will tell you that the practices of their religion are the absolute truth, as they have been proven by the Prophets of their religion and recorded in the doctrines. Though each person holds their religion beliefs and believes the teachings of their religion to be the absolute truth, there are a million other religious teachings out there. There is no one proven truth so who is right and who is wrong? Or course, the answer to that question, in the mind of the believer is, *"I am right, you are wrong."*

In the West, we are bombarded by a mishmash of varying religious cultures and beliefs. So much so that here, religious ideologies have become an intermingled mess. Certainly, Christianity, in its varying forms, is the dominate religious of this culture but people seek answers, they want to believe that they have a purpose, that there is something more, so they turn to those who promise these answers, opening the door to financing the lifestyle and stroking the ego of many a False Prophet.

Generally, when we are young, there is a belief system programmed into our minds. This is most likely the religion of our parents. Some hold fast to these beliefs throughout their life, others do not; they seek something more. The one thing I can tell you about this practice, as I too am one who sought other things, is that due to the childhood programming there is something that has been embedded so deeply into our psyche that no matter where we go, what we study, the games of dress-up we play, at our core is that religious ideology. I have watched so many people as they were preparing to leave their physical body, near the time of their death, revert to their original religion. This, even though some had spent the better part of their lifetime claiming to be, believing that they believed in something else.

In fact, when spirituality and human growth was at its height, in the 1960s and 1970s, it was often taught how one had to consciously let go of all of their childhood programming. Though this may be a nice thought, it is virtually impossible.

So, for better or for worse, we are what we were taught as children. Yes, our minds expand, yes we come upon new ideologies and philosophic concepts that we may like, and we may even encounter new religions that we may even believe in, but at the end of our life we are bound by the beliefs that were indoctrinated into us in childhood.

Throughout history religions have evolved. The Christianity that was practiced two thousand years ago is not the same as it is practiced today. This is the same with all other world religions and even the lessor known or long forgotten ones. What does this tell us? It tells us that the Buddhists of the first century were taught, believed, and practiced their religion very differently than they do today, just as is the case with Christians, Muslims, and so on. The basis of their beliefs may still be in place: i.e. the Bible, the Koran, or the Dharmapada, but, via the mind of man, the teachings of these religions have expanded, evolved, and, in fact, been guided by the desires of man.

It is very easy to study the evolution of Christianity. Documents are everywhere. You can trace how what we know as the Bible came to be fortified and how the teachings and the practices of Christianity came to formulated. What do you see when you study this evolution? You see the mind of a man or a group of people deciding what they thought Christianity should be. And, this is the case from this religion's inception forward. Jesus did not write the bible. His disciples did after he had died or ascended depending on how you want to look at it. As it was formulated in the minds of man, based upon their own personal remembrances, visions, and desires, how does that make it holy? Certainly, the zealots will say that they were guided by the hand of god and stuff like that. But, were they? Look at Christianity's evolution, it was based upon power grabs and desire. And, this is not just the case of Christianity, study the evolution of the other world religions, as well. All are based in the desire of man proclaiming that they know the appropriate interpretation of the teachings and the scriptures.

So, what does this leave us with? It leaves us believing in something that we were programmed to believe — something that we were told was the truth and was holy but it was simply formulated in the mind of man. Yet, at our inner core, we are damned to believe it. It is inside of us.

So, who makes this stuff up? Some guy… Why do we believe it? We have no choice. What can we do about this phenomenon? I have no idea. But, you should think about it before you believe what you believe.

* * *

17/05/16 15:51

Is the message you speak your own or did you hear it from someone else?

If you initially heard it from someone else, then you owe them for every word you speak.

Who do you owe?

Trolling for Dollars
17/05/16 15:50

I listened to a fairly interesting report on NPR today as I was driving back from Hollywood. It was about this one female politician who had gotten trolled pretty hard. They brought in a person who was an expert on the subject. She detailed how the people who troll do so for a number of reasons: insecurity, self-anger, a way to make themselves feel empowered, a means to channel the anger they feel towards life due to their lack of accomplishment, and so on. It was all the psychologically based reasons that we would assume causes a person go on the troll.

Having been trolled myself, once or twice, I find the focused actions of these people very curious. I mean sure, we all have our anger, we all have our likes and our dislikes, we all have our desire to live a better, more fulfilled life but most of us who experience these feelings do something to actualize a better existence. We try to make our life better. We do not waste our time attacking someone for a reason only harbored in our own mind or in the misplaced consciousness of a cyber group that we frequent.

One of the people on the program discussed how a troll had actually set up a twitter account using her dead father's name and just struck out at her in the vilest ways. I mean, I would question who is even so low to do something that? The fact is, it's messed up, but there are people out there who do that kind of stuff. Eventually, this lady wrote an article about this troll and the effect he was having on her life. Apparently, the guy read the article, contacted her, and told her how he never realized all the pain he was causing, as he never thought of her as a person. He apologized and they spoke for hours.

This, of course, is the ideal end to being trolled but I would bet this rarely, if ever, happens. People out there trolling are anonymous; they are out there lying about who they are. And, like this guy before he had his mystical realization, he didn't even think about this woman as a person, he wanted to hurt her, so he trolled her to the max. Why?

I think that most people like me (especially if they have met me) and understand what I'm doing. So, my troll hits have not been too hard. Like I said in a recent blog, people either say, "Fuck you," or write these articulate pieces that though based upon altered facts and misrepresentations of the truths, are at least well written. Thus, they make me smile. Though they probably do hurt my reputation in the minds of people who actually read that kind of stuff and believe it. But, what can I do? Ultimately, the karma goes back onto those who concocted their words in the first place.

It is important to keep in mind, however, that none of the people who have trolled me have ever asked for my side of the story before instigating their troll. Additionally, they have never woken up, seen that I am a person, and said, *"Sorry,"* or anything else for the mistruths, harsh comments, and lies they have spread about me. And, if they have trolled me, that means they have done it to others. Certainly, I am not all that special, so I am sure they have hit others much harder.

The fact is, tracing an ip addresses is pretty easy. In some cases, I have watched from where these troll hits have arisen. It's pretty easy to know who some of these people are. …Some have even friended me on Facebook. They don't remove the lies that they put out there but they want to be my friend. I think that's pretty strange. I guess they want to see what I'm up to? Weird…

You know, I came up in a world of spirituality. For me, life is all about Karma Yoga — doing for others and asking nothing in return. I realize that the world has changed a lot since then. There was no internet and none of the non-stop babble that goes on via the various cyber space methods. All this being said, think about it; isn't doing something good for other people; saying something good about other people, better than being a troll? I mean, doing something good, helping someone; doesn't that make you feel good?

So, if you're angry, frustrated, insecure, whatever; instead of going on the troll, get up off of your butt and do something positive for someone else. The world then becomes a better place. Be a conduit for positivity. Not a negative troll.

Anyway, like I always talk about… I think the main thing in life is not to focus on other people: what you like or dislike about them, what you like or dislike about what they have done. Instead, never use other people as your basis of suchness. Do something for yourself. Do something that makes you, YOU. Create your own something. And mostly, own who and what you are. If you're going to say something be brave enough to claim it or be adult enough to understand that we each have our own life and our life-missions and say nothing at all.

To the trolls out there, think about it, from the doing something and being something positive you won't be lost in all that insecurity and self-directed anger that makes you troll people in the first place. BECOME and then you won't need to attack and criticize.

BE and YOU are.

He Died and He is Never Coming Back
16/05/16 08:34

This is a very emotional day for me in that this is the first morning I woke up without my best bud of a cat walking on me as an alarm clock, telling me that he decided that it is time for me (and my lady) to wake up. He died yesterday and he is never coming back. So, he is not jumping up and down, on and off of my desk as I type this blog, walking on my keyboard, messing up my spelling, climbing on my lap, and generally bothering me. I loved it and I loved him. It is very sad that he is gone.

For anyone who has ever owned a pet and really cared about them you can understanding the devastating loss of losing them. It just takes your world apart.

The sad thing is, the guy was only seven. Our previous cats have lived until at least fifteen. I purchased him from a breeder up in Ridgecrest, which is a few hours North of L.A., near the end of the Mojave Desert and the beginning of the Sierra Nevada Mountains. It snowed as I reached the higher elevations as I drove there that day. Being from L.A., where it never snows, I thought that was pretty auspicious. When I got to the house, the breeder released the three kittens I had to choose from out of their pen. I was kneeing down and one walked right up my leg and nestled his face into my shirt. My choice was made. He and I drove back down to L.A. and all was well with the world.

Recently, he started to lose weight so we took him to the Vet. The Vet did an ultrasound and discovered he had liver cancer. There was really nothing she could do, so it was pretty devastating, but in previous cases, when our cats were reaching their later days, they would live for months or even a year and they declined very slowly. Thus, we had the chance to see it coming and make their life as good a possible. But, three days ago, on Friday morning, he was fine. He was jumping around. By Saturday morning things began to go down hill fast. As the day went on he began to make these screeching sounds. This, from a cat that rarely spoke. He was obviously in pain. He kept walking around to his favorite spots, laying there for a moment, probably trying to find some solace in a place he loved to sit, and then he would move on. I stayed up with him all Saturday night making sure he didn't go somewhere that he could conformably get down from but by Sunday morning he was trying to walk around, get up and down off of things, but he was very-very shaky.

The problem was, it was Sunday, virtually no Vet is opened. But, I finally found one, explained the situation, and we made an appointment. By this point he could barely move. So, I took him outside onto the patio to let him see the divine mother ocean that he loved so much — he used to sit out there on the patio, basking in the sun, for hours. I let him say goodbye to the succulents that he used to love watching the hummingbirds feed from. That's all I could do… The last gift I could give him.

By the time we got him to the Vet his face was pretty much just buried in the blanket. Gone…

For anyone who has ever lost someone you really care about, maybe you can understand. The sad thing I realized about all of this is that most people who read this will not even care. All they are thinking about is their own moment and though some may feel empathy, in a few seconds they will forget this and move onto thinking about themselves again. This is sadly the largest curse of life I believe, the fact that so few people truly care about others.

I am forever both surprised and happy for a person when I meet someone who has not encountered death. Though it is the most commanding reality of life, I think until you meet it face-to-face, with someone you really care about, you do not know what true emotional pain is. For those who have not been forced into this emotion, I am so happy for them. But, most of us are not that fortunate.

For me, I met it very young. My grandfather passed away on Christmas Eve when I was three. I remember waiting in the hospital all night and then going home to a Christmas tree. Very weird experience... I also had a dog that I really loved when I was seven. As an only child and a latchkey kid that dog was my everything. He died about a year into his life from Korean distemper. As a boy raised in good Christian family, after that, every night when I said my prayers, before I went to bed, I would pray for those who needed help to receive it, ask for forgiveness for my sins, and then I would beg god to give me another dog. Fifty years later, still no dog. So much for praying...

I actually had a dog before that when was I maybe two. I had gotten the croup and I remember my dog visiting me in my crib. (Yes, I know it's weird but I can remember back to when I was very young). When I had gotten better I ask my mother, from my crib, if she could bring the dog to visit. She told me it had gotten my croup and died. I was devastated. The fact is, that thought always haunted me — that I had killed my dog. It wasn't until I was in my mid-thirties that I realized, dogs don't get croup. My mother had lied to me. My parents had just wanted to get rid of the dog. Obviously, she was one of those people who should never have been allowed to be a parent.

My father died when I was ten and my life totally went to shit after that. I always felt for my paternal grandmother as she lost her husband and two of her three children while she was still alive; one right after the other. That had to be very hard.

I watched as some of the people I was close to die at the hands of violence in my younger years. I had one friend die of lung cancer at thirty-two and another from prostate cancer at thirty-eight. ...Both way too young to die from those diseases. I had close family members die in the Vietnam War for absolutely no reason. Think about it, this government drafted kids and sent them to war at eighteen before they could even legally drink and you couldn't even vote until you twenty-one back then. How wrong is that and how many people died for nothing? Very sad.

When I was in high school I had this friend who was the first guy to get into vintage guitars that I knew of. And, this was the 70s before anyone was into them. He died right after graduation in a motorcycle wreck. I had met his parents and they were older; retired military. I always thought that had to be devastating to lose your only child when there is so little left of life.

I know… This kind of sound like the Jim Carrol song, *"People who died."* Sorry…

As for me, I never thought I would make it this far. I am a decade older than my father or my maternal grandfather ever lived to be. I figured I would probably have walked down the wrong backstreet in Asian somewhere and gotten jacked by this point. Though it did happen more than once, for whatever reason, I was the one to walk away with only the scares left to document the experience.

So many people and so many of my animal friends have passed away… That is just the curse of age, I guess. The older you get; the more death you are forced to encounter.

The fact is, it is easy to be nonchalant about death. It is easy to be philosophic. It is easy to only think about yourself and not care about the pain others are going through due to someone dying that they cared about. It's all easy, until someone you really care about dies. Then, when you are in the middle of the emotion, it is not so easy. You understand how important life is.

Rest in Peace my little buddy. You will forever be in my heart.

As You Remember It or As It Was Lived
14/05/16 08:32

Most people do not have the mental aptitude to:

1) Be honest and truthful to others
2) Be honest and truthful to themselves
3) To tell a story as it truly happened and not embellish it to make themselves look better.

Life is lived as we have lived it. Life is then recorded in our brains. From our brains, the life as we have lived it is then interpreted and told to others. The problem arises in the interpretation of what was lived.

Each person has their own psychological make-up. They each possess their own set of desires and they each want to be seen in a certain light. Some people set about accomplishing their dreams, others do not. From both of these cases there arises the need to alter the facts of reality to make an individual be perceived in a particular manner.

Those who seek achievement work hard to gain that achievement. As they walk down this path, many times they feel the need to embellish what they have done to add to the perception that they are climbing up the ladder. Those who have not achieved, commonly attempt to walk one of two roads. One, they attempt to link themselves to those that have achieved so that they can bask in their limelight. Two, as they have no sense of personal achievement they attempt to cast doubt about those who have actually achieved in order to draw themselves into the center of the conversation.

Think about your own life. One, has there been times when you were working towards achieving something and you wanted to make your achievement look grander than it actually was so you altered the facts as you told the story about your accomplishment? Two, has there been a time when you have been working towards something, asked someone else to join in, and then they found a nonsensical reason to attack you and spread their misplaced beliefs to the world? They did nothing, yet they attempted to drag you down. In each case, there was the truth about what actually occurred and then there was the personal interpretation of that truth.

Moving from simply what is projected to the world, (to come to understand the reason why), look deeply into yourself. Think about some-thing; an event that happened in your life. First, find an event where you clearly know what happened and why, yet you changed the facts when you told the story to other people. Define, why did you do that? Do not simply dismiss this as a mental exercise; actually look deeply into your own personal psyche and come to a clear conclusion of why you did it. Why did you do it?

Once you have established that fact about your mental make-up, scan your memories and think about a time when you lived an experience involving another person. Find a time when a person either invited you into a project or perhaps you simply decided to focus on that person for some interpersonal reason. Perhaps you became very infatuated with that individual or perhaps you became mad at them. In either case, it is essential to look deeply within yourself and find out why you became involved with that person in the first place. Why did you do it? What did it mean to you? And, what was your desired outcome? Once this fact is clearly defined in your mind, spell out why you then became infatuated or angry with that person. Clearly come to this conclusion. At this point, chart what you said to others about that individual and why. Was what you spoke the truth or was it simply the truth from your point of view? How did you alter the facts of the situation to cast your own personalized perspective about this person to the others you spoke to? Why did you do it? And, what did you hope would happen to and for your life by doing it?

It is essential, if you hope to come to a deeper understanding about yourself, as you pass through this life, that you do not simply cast these memories, based upon physical interactions, to the realms of wandering mind stuff. Who you are today is based upon what you thought, what you did, and what you spoke yesterday. Who you will be tomorrow is based upon what you did and what you said today.

Ask yourself, do you base your life upon truth? Is that truth only your truth, as you interpret events, or is it the absolute truth? If you do not base your life upon the actual truth, if you alter, reword, and reintellectualize the truth to make yourself look better and be the center of the conversation than you will continually be deceived throughout your lifetime. Why? Because the truth is born from you. If you speak the truth, with no altercations based upon personal desires, then all you say will equal all you become.

Has your interpretation of the truth hurt someone? Has your reinterpretation of the truth made you greater or lessor? Both of these questions lead to who and what you are; who and what you will become.

If you project falsehoods, all you will be left with is lies. How do you choose to live?

If You Are Not an Adult
13/05/16 07:16

When one is young they want to be seen as an adult. They want to make their own decisions, control their own life, and do the things that they what to do when they want to do them. For those of us who have lived life for a longer period of time I am sure that we can all remember back to our early years when we struggled to become who we wanted to be. For those progressing though that stage of their life right now I am sure that many of you are encounter the obstacles that come from not being your own person, living under the jurisdiction of your family.

For some, living with their family is a method to keep themselves from being forced into the job market; doing the nine-to-five at a job they do not really like. As some parents are more lenient than others, many a young person lives with their parents' way longer than they should. Though many will justify their reason for doing this, there is one fact that is undeniable, if you are not living on your own; paying your own rent or mortgage, paying for your transportation: be it a car, a bike, or a subway token, if you are not paying your own bills you are not an adult. Yes, you may be old enough to smoke, drink, and vote but if you are not on your own, you are not on your own.

There comes a responsibility with being a true, functioning adult. You have to do what it takes to survive. You have to do what you do to get your rent and your grocery bill paid. Though you may not like the job you have, you do it because that is the cost of living the life of an adult.

So many people in this modern era of the free world hide from this fact. So many people lie to themselves. So many people justify their deeds and actions. But, lies and justifications is all that it is. If you are not on your own, paying your own bills, you are not an adult.

So, what is the point of this conversation?

People go out into the world and present themselves as adults. They go out there and do what they do, cast judgments, speak their mind, interact with others, and have all of the desires that we all possess. But, if they are not a functioning adult what do these actions and opinions really detail about an individual? What they detail is that they are living a lie. They are not responsible enough to be able to take care of themselves and, as such, what they say and what they do should be seen as such.

Compare how you think and feel about a person who has their own place to one who is living with their parents past the point of being a teenager. For most of us, that definition who be delineated by the fact that one would be considered a dependent while the other is a functioning adult. With that standing comes a lot more respect.

Who do you respect? Commonly, you respect a person who has done something good, providing a positive service to the world, while embracing the fact that they did it while holding their own in a completive and rarely fair world.

For those of us who have lived the life of an adult for a day, a month, a year, or for decades, we understand the reality of reality. You must make your own way or no one will respect you. For the young who still live under the roof of their parents or are financed by their family funds, you can deceive yourself but think about what your parents had to do to provide a life and a lifestyle for you. They had to do what it took to make a buck. They were adults.

At each stage of our life we have a choice about what we will do now and what we will do next. If you are young, this is your time to make the right choice. Don't pretend to be an adult, actually become an adult. For this is the place were all long-term self-worth and gaining the respect of others is given birth to.

* * *

12/05/16 08:51

If someone doesn't care you can spend your entire life attempting to make them care but they never will.

* * *

12/05/16 08:43

You can get down on your knees and pray to god for help or you can get up off your knees and go and do something that will actually help.

Filing a Complaint
12/05/16 08:37

Have you ever filed a complaint against someone and soon after that your life began to take a turn for the worse? Why is that?

The answer is very simple. People file complaints because <u>they</u> are unhappy with the way <u>they</u> were treated, with what <u>they</u> received for their payment, or <u>their</u> dissatisfaction with an overall experience. At the root of this equation is one person being unhappy and blaming their unhappiness upon another.

With this as a basis, lets look into this a little further. A person (maybe you) made a choice to do something. Though they were the one to make the choice to purchase something or participate in an event, they do not want to take responsibility for that choice. They do not want to take responsibility for the choice they made and, thus, they attempt to blame someone else for their dissatisfaction.

No matter what you thought you would receive, no matter what you were promised, it was you who made the choice to partake. As it was you who made that choice, it is one-hundred percent your responsibility that you were involved in the exchange — whatever that exchange may have been. Thus, if it is you who makes a compliant against another person, you are thereby directly affecting the life and the livelihood of that other person. As you are the one unhappy, by filing that complaint, and negatively affecting another person's life, who do you think will ultimately suffer and pay the karma — you will? For, it was <u>you</u> who made the choice to do something and then it was <u>you</u> who didn't like the experience, and then it was <u>you</u> who instigating that complaint. The number one factor in this equation is, *"You."*

There is a funny commercial in rotation on the radio right now. It is advertising a service to get people out of a timeshare that they bought. It states, you don't have to live with your mistakes like when you invested all of your savings in a dot com startup in 1999.

As you may know, there was a big investment frenzy in the late 1990s regarding the dot com boom. A lot of people, hoping to get rich overnight, lost their investments when the dot com bubble burst. But again, who's fault was it? Was it the dot com industry or the person who believed that they would make a lot of money by wildly investing? Obviously, it was the ladder.

People never want to take responsibly for their actions. They choose to do something but then, when they don't like it, they want to blame someone else. This is a very selfish and unthinking mindset, because by blaming someone else you instigate an entire world of unknown karma coming your direction. You chose to do something. You didn't like the outcome. You complained in order to get your money back or to pretend the experience was never lived; but it was. You made a choice. Thus, that choice is your responsibility. No one else's. As it is your responsibility, if you attempt to turn that responsibility to someone else, your life will suffer, as you have hurt the life of another person who may or may not be responsible for your dissatisfaction.

It is important that you think about this. You want to live a better life; your happiness begins with the choices you make. Be responsible for them and do not attempt to blame someone else.

Right is Right, Wrong is Wrong, the World of Political Correctness, and Who is Really to Blame?
11/05/16 09:33

As each of us pass through life we watch as the trends; what is acceptable and what is not acceptable, change. What is right in one era and in one culture is taboo in another. From our position in culture and in history we all pass judgment about what others are doing: what they have done, why they have done it, and who is to blame. This is especially the case when we, ourselves, have encountered bad actions done to us by the hands of others.

People do wrong things; I have, you have, we all have. If we can get ourselves together enough to look at the causation factors for why we have done these bad things and find some internal and/or external guidance, then maybe we can become better and not do bad things again. Maybe…

As has been long documented, the abusers were once the abused, the criminals commonly grew up in a world surrounded by destitution and crime. When we are young, and perhaps still involved with or haunted by that which we went through, change for the better is very difficult. In fact, many of us are kept from gaining the help we need due those around us who hold us locked into a negative mindset and lifestyle.

As the world of political correctness and judgment have grown, hand-in-hand with this people have used these ideologies to step back into time and find a reason to blame others for what was done to them. They do this before they ever consider the reason why an action was enacted. Though there is never an excuse for doing things that hurt another person, there are definitely causation factors.

For us, who walk the path of consciousness, it is important that we take these factors into consideration before we cast blame. Just as we each have done bad things, bad things have, undoubtedly, been done to all of us. We can focus on those things, we can hate the person who did them, showing no levels of understanding or forgiveness, or we can choose to raise ourselves to a higher level of consciousness and come into the space of empathy. We should do this because, the fact is, the person who hurt you was undoubtedly hurt in a similar way by someone else, just as the people you have hurt were damaged by you enacting some form of hurtful negativity that was directed at you in the past. Never an excuse, just a fact.

We all are defined by what we have lived through. Some of us have unfortunately lived through a lot more pain, both physical and psychological, than others. As this is the case, we must all learn to stop blaming and stop being defined by our past. We must find the help and the guidance that we need and rise ourselves to a new and better level of consciousness not defined by our previous experiences but by the positivity we can bring to the world: right here, right now.

Forgive and forget. Enter a new realm of freedom.

Out With the New In With the Old
11/05/16 08:40

Back in the early 80s I picked up a Casio MT40 when they first hit the market. These were pretty much the first mini-keyboard, with a variety of sounds, and a built in drum machine to be released. They were really cool! I remember picking mine up at Guitar Center in Hollywood and purchasing the plastic hard shell case that went along with it. I think it cost me a little over a hundred bucks back then. I toyed with it a lot in the early days and even used it on a couple of recordings as it sounded really cool. As time went on, Casio began to release slightly bigger versions of the mini-keyboard. I remember some L.A. bands and musicians like Sue Tissue of the *Suburban Lawns* even playing one onstage.

Time went on and the mini-keyboards and their offshoots became more-and-more advanced. Though I too moved along with the times, for some reason that original MT40 is still in my possession. I can't even tell you why as through the years I gave away, threw away, or sold pretty much all of my equipment from that era. But, there it is…

Now, I had not played it for years, (decades), as it runs on batteries and/or a weird voltage power converter that I no longer had. So, it just sat around, hiding in closet or something. A couple of days ago I was in a thrift store and low-and-behold there was the Casio power converter, made for this unit, still in its original box. They were charging the whopping high price of $1.99 for it. Of course, I purchased it. I took it home, grabbed the MT40, popped open the case and there it was, the mini-keyboard still in pristine condition. I plugged it in, tuned it on, and it works perfectly — just like when it was new.

As you may know, sometimes electronic items, even though they are not used, die via the hands time. But, not this MT40.

Though the times have changed and electronics have advanced beyond belief, it is really cool to sit back into the distance of time and play some music on what was so cutting edge back then. Creating music of a time gone past…

Maybe You Will or Maybe You Won't
10/05/16 07:07

I was speaking with this very successful writer yesterday that I have known for a few years and he asked me an interesting question, *"Who reads your blog?"* I told him that I don't really know — except for the people who contact me when the blog is on hiatus and ask me to recommence, I really have no idea — though I do know the numbers are pretty big.

He then, with a bit of a snarky attitude, asked me, *"Why do people read your blog?"* I told him I don't really have an answer for that either. I turned the questioning back on him, (knowing that he has read my blog), *"Why do you read it?"* He said he liked my weird perceptions of life and the way I tie them to philosophy. Okay, sounds good to me...

He then told me, with a bit of a condescending tone, if he wrote a blog a million people would read it. Not being a person who is prone to envy or jealousy this made me smile and I asked him, why didn't he then. He told me he was so successful that he needed to be paid for any words he put to paper. This also made me smile as I have known so many people, especially in the film and music business, who at one point in their life were so successful and now they live in a dumpy apartment, are couch surfing, or are back at home living with their parents waiting for them to die so they can inherent the house. In other words, being successful today is no guarantee you will be successful tomorrow.

But, all of this got me thinking about the blog... Personally, I have always enjoyed reading autobiographies, interviews, and autobiographic recollections put to literature as it always provides me with a way to come to understand how a person thinks and how they view and interact with life. Though I may not always agree with their life-perceptions, I forever find them interesting as it provides me with food for thought. And, I think that's what this blog is about. I don't do this for a living, like some bloggers do, I don't ask for donation (though you can give them to me if you want to ☺), I don't seek disciples or converts, I am just a guy presetting some food for thought; tied to experiences I have lived in my life.

As a person, I always try to see things through the eyes of positivity, happiness, and humor. I am a terrible joker. I always make jokes and try to present things in a humorous vein wherever I communicate. As something is often lost in translation, especially when it is written, (as we all know from our emails or texts that may have been misinterpreted), I understand that some people may not see that I am smiling, (and possibly making a joke), when I write certain things. But, that's just life in cyberspace. That's why I always prefer face-to-face conversations rather than via the internet. But, the internet is what we have. The tool of the devil… The tool of all of us who write and do not charge money to read. …Who just do it as a possible means to help humanity in any small way that we can.

So, I hope everyone who reads this blog takes something positive away from it. Maybe it gives you some food for thought about how you can make your own life a little bit better and find a better way to live while overcoming some of life's obstacles. Maybe you will maybe you won't… Or, maybe it will just provide you with a look at the experiences of another person to see that we all go through similar nonsense in this place we call life.

But mostly, I hope it makes you smile. ☺

But You've Done Something Wrong
09/05/16 07:47

Recently, I've been focusing on studying the interaction of people to other people and the way in which people interact with the greater world around themselves. This hasn't been so much by choice but it has been due to the interactions that have undesirously been brought into my life.

For each of us, as we pass through our life-time, there will be periods when all is calm and well. Then, there will be times when we encounter situations that we wish we did not. Though we hope for these segments of our life to be kept to a minimal, I believe that for those of us who care enough to study existence that these encounters provide a true insight into the make-up of life. From this, we can learn and become better, more whole individuals.

People do things that are wrong. This is a simple fact of life. We all do things that are wrong. For most of us these are small mistakes that we didn't actually mean to do. For others, they chart their whole life by going from one act of wrongness that leads to another and to another. We can all question, *"Why?"* But, the answer only lies within the individual. And, for those who behave in this manner, I believe that they are made up of the mindset that they do not even care what they do, why they do it, or whom they injure in the process.

Can you change the mind of that type of a person, I don't know? Perhaps only if something truly cataclysmic happens to them and from that they may begin to rethink their life.

Wrongs can be small or they can be large. The large ones are generally acted out when a person has thought them through, set up a plan, and then executed that plan. The small one are more based in happenstance. But, it is essential to note that happenstance is instigated by the mind of the person.

For example, yesterday I was heading out to breakfast with my lady. We were leading to this Japanese restaurant we enjoy. It has a great outdoor space and they do great latte' art. En route, I encounter a car that was stopped at a stop sign. The only problem was the car was stationed halfway between the main lane and the right turn lane where I hoped to turn right. No one else was in the intersection so I pulled up behind them and after sitting there for a few moments I gave them a little tap on the horn to alert them to the fact that someone else was behind them. Nothing happened. They didn't move. As they were an SUV and I couldn't really see around them, I assumed someone must be walking through the intersection. As those few seconds, that feel like eternity, passed by, the SUV finally moved. As they did, they flipped me off. No one was in the intersection, they simply decided they didn't like me alerting them to the fact that other people are in this world and they had the right to do anything that they want.

As I am often amused by the ridiculousness of life and the way people behave this act made me smile but it also hit the anger spot in me. *"What an asshole,"* I thought.

You see, this is where the small wrongs of life lead to the big wrongs of life. This is where a minor mistake can escalate. The fact is, if you behave in this manner (anywhere/anyplace in life) it can grow and define your greater reality. I mean, there is always someone bigger and better than you. Just like the gunfighters of the Old West, there is always someone faster. And, if you behave in a confrontational manner, confrontation will find you and sooner-or-later you will meet your superior.

As a funny sidebar… Back when I used to live overlooking Hermosa Beach, I would drive to *The Original Farmers Market* a couple of days a week for breakfast or lunch. My lady would joke, *"You go there every day."*

Though I didn't, it was funny because driving to central L.A. from the South Bay was quite a distance. Plus, we would drive to Huntington Beach to go to the gym every night. Again, quite a distance. But, back then, traffic was not so bad. As long as you weren't driving in the crunch time it was twenty minutes or so each direction. Now, traffic in L.A. is insane, just a decade or two later. There are so many cars you can't get anywhere. And, even when you're driving through a relatively uncrowded beach community like I was yesterday, you encounter drivers like the aforementioned SUV.

This brings us to the question of life... When you do something wrong, do you own it? Most of us do. We say, *"Excuse me," "Sorry,"* or if we are driving we give the other driver a friendly wave. But, there are others, who instead of taking the time to think about another person, they either try to change the subject, turn the truth around and attempt to make the other person look wrong, (even when they've done nothing wrong), or, as in the case of the SUV driver, attempt to turn a meaningless, minor situation into a confrontation. Why? Why can't some people care enough to care? Why can't some people own the truth? They did something wrong; say, *"I'm sorry."*

This makes me think back to when I was in grad school. I had this one class and one of the assignments was to write a paper studying the work of this one author who rose to public prominence in the 1960s. Prior to taking the class I had read much of his work and I was really not fond of his approach. I felt he took facts from here and there and turned them into a mishmash designed to draw in the reader to a reality concocted only in his own mind. But, he presented his work as fact. Thus, that is what my paper addressed. My instructor, however, did not like my approach. She returned my paper, believing it was too opinionated and not scholastic, and made me rewrite it. It was a twenty-five-page, annotated, paper so this was not an easy task. But, from this experience it truly made me realize how people choose to define the world by their own set of beliefs. From this, they attempt to cast their beliefs about life and/or other people onto the world. But, that is false. This is not reality. This is only opinion. And, if you do this about other people, what does that say about you? What it says about you is that you may be wrong. And, if you are wrong then you set an entire course of negative events into motion based upon a choice you made, in your own mind, to cast a judgment about a person or a life event.

I have always kept a copy of that original paper as it truly helped me realize a lot about life…

Most people do not have the level of mentorship as I did with my instructor, however. They encounter life guided simply my what they think, how they feel, and then they are supported by a group of people who feel the same way and think the same thoughts. At most, some attempt to cover up their misplaced options with biased facts that they obtain from apparent factual sources, just like I did with my paper. But, these are just the projection of opinion appearing to be facts. They are thoughts about a subject, not necessary the right thoughts, simply the thoughts instigated by one person and then spread to the masses.

So, who are you? What do you do? How do you encounter life? Are you judgmental? Do you instigate confrontation when there need be none? Or, are you enlightened enough to recognize when you are wrong? And, when you are wrong, do you care enough about other people and the world around you to say, *"I'm sorry,"* and undo what you have done?

*   *   *

08/05/16 14:11

When someone that you know dies do you believe that they watch over you from the great beyond? When are they watch, when are they not? Do you really want someone observing all of the actions you perform here on earth?

The Worship of Falsehood
07/05/16 08:18

I often write about and discuss the fact that so much of what people believe comes from where? It comes from the mind of man. Yet, it is claimed to be divine inspiration or something based in the gospels.

People spend their entire life believing. Now, I am not saying that is a bad thing. I am simply asking the question, *"Where does the bases of your beliefs arise?"* Most people never take the time to think about this.

If you believe what you believe, great! But, for me, I like to know the source.

I think to the works of Carlos Castaneda... Now, I must preface this with the fact that I think that Carlos Castaneda rocks. I mean he received a Master Degree and a Ph.D. from U.C.L.A. based upon a thesis and dissertation that he (more or less) completely made up. How cool is that! He totally messed with the system and I think that is great! This being said, when his works began to be published, they were consumed by 1970s culture and people really took to them, believing what he said to be the truth. But, what did he say? He claimed what he wrote was based upon the teachings he received from a Yaqui Shaman but it was basically just him spouting wisdom as he interpreted it in his own mind.

I was lucky enough to have a chance encounter with Carlos Castaneda many years ago, he seemed like a nice, reserved man. By then, the talk, for those of us who have our ears to the ground, was afoot that what he wrote wasn't factual. But, does it really matter? I mean whether it was the teachings of Lao Tzu, Joseph Smith, L. Ron Hubbard, or whoever else all of this stuff that his been referred to as religious gospel came from, it was based in the mind of a man who then presented it to the world. So, who's to say what is right and what is wrong? Who's to say what is factual? You believe what you believe.

This being the case, the point I am trying to make is belief is a dangerous sword. What you believe is what you believe. But, why do you believe it?

Take a second right now and think about this. Look to your deepest inner-beliefs and question, *"Where do those beliefs come from?"* The answer will be a little different for each person but ultimately it is you who chooses to believe what you believe.

Now that you have that first answer as a basis, ask yourself, *"Does it matter to you if what you believe is true gospel? Or, are you okay with believing simply the words that came out of the mind of a man?"*

*   *   *

07/05/16 07:34

Just because you buy a pair of shoes that are too big does not mean that your feet have grown.

* * *

07/05/16 07:31

Do you do things that hurt other people based upon what you like and what you don't like, who you like and who you don't like? Are you willing to undo what you have done? If you aren't, you will forever be damned by your actions as you are the one who set everything in motion guided only by a concept based in your own mind.

* * *

06/05/16 08:17

Are you happy?

If not, why not?

What would make you happy?

As long as being happy is based upon something you don't have, you will never have it.

* * *

06/05/16 08:16

Right now, in this moment, who are you thinking about and why?

* * *

06/05/16 08:15

When was the last time that you said you were sorry and meant it?

* * *

06/05/16 08:14

If you are basing your life on anger how do you ever expect to find any peace?

* * *

06/05/16 08:12

When was the last time you did something nice for someone and did it for no reason?

Inspiration from the Obscene
06/05/16 07:39

In each of our lives there comes a time when somebody enters our existence and they really mess things up. Sometime these encounters only last for a moment. In other cases, these interactions have the potential to define many years of our life. In either case, we don't want the negative experiences brought on by our interactions with this individual to have ever happened but, this is life, and at times we all encounter negative life experiences delivered to us by someone else.

In some cases, we invite these individuals into our life. We meet them, they may seem nice or appear as if they have something to give to our life that we desire. In other cases, they force their way into our lives in a way that we never hoped-for, desired, or have any responsibility for. These forced interactions can come from any number of causes: another employee at the workplace, someone moves into your neighborhood, an unconscious driver smashes into you with their car, and the list goes on. But, at the root of any of these defining factors is the element that the person enters your existence and things are never the same — they are worse.

Once this person enters your life and they mess things up, it is common to harbor a lot of frustration, dissatisfaction, and anger towards this person. They came in, they messed things up, and you are the one left dealing with the consequences. Commonly, a person who unleashes negativity is so lost to the true realms of higher consciousness and reality that they do not even care who they have hurt and never set about on a course to make it right. In fact, they may even blame you. Wrong, but it is seen as right in their distorted mind.

So, what can you do?

The fact is, there is no hard answer for what you can do as once these encounters take place each person's life is damaged in a different way. Though you may want revenge, as a conscious individual you will probably never pursue that path. This being said, the one thing that you can do is gain inspiration from the obscene. The first thing you must establish is the villain in the equation. And, if you have personally made the mistake of letting that person into your life, you must draw the boundaries; stop the interaction(s) if you can or, at least, limit the interactions if they are, for example, a coworker or a neighbor. Then, you must study that person: watch them, listen to them, remember their actions; what they did and did not do; what they said and how they behaved. Once you have done this, you, as a conscious person, who truly wishes to make you and the world a better place, must then take what you have witnessed in this person and use it to guide you to never do what they have done.

Never let your actions hurt anyone else. And, if you have intentionally or accidentally hurt someone in your past do all that you can do to undo what you have done and fix what you have broken.

The mark of caring conscious individual is caring enough to care.

The Process of Realization
05/05/16 07:58

Most people never take the time to study why the behave the way they behave. They simply pass through their life giving no thought to the process of personal realization.

Commonly, people know they have a personality and that they feel a certain way or behave in a particular manner when they are reacting to the various stimuli they encounter in life but they never take the time to study why they behave in this manner. At best, they simply write it off to the excuse, *"That's just who I am."*

But, why are you who you are? Why do you behave the way you behave, do the things you do, and act out in the manner in which you act out? If you do not know the answers to these questions you are living your life from a place where no personal realization can ever be had. You are living in a place where your emotions control your every move and can lead you down the road to alienating other people, damaging the lives of others and your own.

When some are confronted with these certainties they write it off to the fact that they do not care about truly knowing themselves — they do care about inner knowledge, all they care about is feeling okay a much of the time as possible and when they do not then their reactions, however hurtful or antisocial they may be, are called for. But, this is simply an excuse not a conscious realization.

This is the place in life that defines who a person truly is and what they can give back to others. For if a person does not care enough to define their own inner motivations they have no possibility of ever gaining control over them and raising to the higher levels of human understanding.

The world begins with you. The world begins with how you interact with the world. Your encounters, relationships, and ultimate life accomplishment are defined by how you act, react, and behave in the presence of others.

If you do not take the time to know who you are and why, life simply becomes a random mess of chance encountered dominated by whatever emotion you are feeling at the moment.

    Your life. Your choice. It all begins with you. But, it only truly begins when you understand who you actually are.

* * *

05/05/16 07:56

What does it mean when you criticize something someone else has created? It means that you've decided that you know more than the creator. But, how is the possible? As it is not your creation you have no understanding of the factors that when into its creation.

The I Don't Care About the I Don't Care
04/05/16 09:35

Let's face facts, nobody cares about you. No one cares about what's going on in your life, what you are going through, and/or what you are feeling. They only pretend to care when they have a reason to pretend to care.

This may sound synclinal but it is not. Think about it, who cares about you? Name the list of people who you believe truly care about you. Now, define why each of these people cares about you. What do you come up with? Your answer will most likely be, they only care about you for and because of a specific reason. If you were not in the position you are in: family or otherwise, friend or otherwise, lover or otherwise, idol or otherwise, would they give you two thoughts? Probably not. Thus, people only care about you if they are forced to care about you or have a self-serving reason to care about you.

Let's look to the bigger picture. There is a whole world of people out there struggling to survive. Do they care about you? No. They care about themselves and those who can help them to survive. Are you one of the people who helps them to survive? Probably not. Thus, they do not care about you.

On the smaller level, people want to do whatever they want to do. They don't care about who's life they affect as long as they are doing what they want to do. They expect there to be no consequence for what they do. When they encounter consequences, when they encounter someone throwing a road block in the way of their doing what they want to do, then they care about the person in a negative manner by becoming angry at that person and for some this means lashing out at that person. The fact is, they care about this person because that person has made them angry and stopped them from doing what they want to do. But, is that truly caring? I don't think so. This is simply the selfish mindset that leads to all of the problems of this world.

Life is a selfish place. Think about your own behavior. Who do you care about and why? Just like you did for those you believe care about you, make a list of the people you care about and then define why you care about each of them. What do you come up with? Do you care about anybody for no reason at all? Probably not. There is a specific reason for why you care about each person you care about.

Life is your choice. How you behave in life is your choice. How you interact with others in life is your choice. What you do, what you say, and how you treat others is your choice. Who you care about and why you care about them is your choice.

This being said, do you want to be a better you? To do this, you need to consciously understand the realities of your existence. You need to define how you feel and why. Once you do this you can then step out into the world with a more defined realization about human interactions and why you feel the way you feel, leading to you behaving in a more conscious manner.

If you do something that makes someone happy, they care about you. If you do something that makes someone angry, they care about you. But, at the root of this caring is the emotion born of the desire of a specific individual to feel a particular way. Selfish, yes. But, this is life.

So, who are you going to be? Are you going to be the person who cares about a person and tries to help them and make their life better only if they make you feel good? Or, are you going to care enough about other people to realize that they each possess their own basis for their reality and care about them just to care?

Payment for My Sins
04/05/16 07:40

For fun, I sometimes post copies of the checks I receive for residual payments from a movie or a T.V. show I did on Facebook, Google+, or on this blog. I do this when the check is in the amount of like five cents. I mean, come on... It costs more to mail it then the amount of the check! I always find that amusing...

Today, I received a royalty check from one of my publishers for $3.03. That's kind of funny too.

Everybody thinks when you write a book, immediately you are rich. ...If you've been in a movie or on a T.V. show, immediately you are rich. No... Though I think the actor's unions and the publishers are cool when they actually hold up their end of the bargain and send out the checks, (because many of them don't). But, the fact is, there is always someone else making the big bucks not the person doing the work.

Sure, if you're Stephen King or J.K Rawlings, and your writings, (and the movies made from them), have made billions of dollars, you can demand a very high price up front, but most of us aren't in that boat. And, the publishers and the productions companies know it. Hell, it is near impossible to get a book deal in today's publishing market unless you are an established author. Due to this fact, many would-be authors take the road of self-publishing and make virtually no money at all. Yet, by self-publishing they can, at least, claim they have a book out there. But, as someone who has walked down the road and worked with a lot of publishing companies, I can tell you that self-publishing is a very different beast than that of actually being published by an established publishing company. In the realm of self-publishing there are no checks and balances, no fact checks, no checking for possible legal issues, no editorial approval.

This is not the case with actual publishing companies, however.

This makes me think back to a funny/interesting story about one of my publishing deals... I wrote, *The Warrior is Silent: Martial Arts and the Spiritual Path.* When the Senior Acquisitions Editor at the company that published it first read the manuscript, he contacted me, he loved it and told me it was the best book on the martial arts he had ever read. Great! I signed the deal. He then sent it over to his Editorial Department. (Of course, this process takes in excess of a year). When I got the manuscript back for final review, the person who did the editing had done the politically correct thing (at least, so they believed) and changed all the *"He,"* (referring to the masses), to an interchangeable *"He or She."* I though this made the book a very hard read. I hated it! So, I contacted the Senior Editor. He said he would take care of it and have the person who actually edited the book call me. A week or so later I get a call. I immediately could tell that the woman was in a very bad mood. I asked her if something was wrong. She told me she had just been fired and this was her last day. Oh great, I thought... I told her of my concerns, she promised she would correct it and that was that. A few months later, I get the book hot off the press. He and She, no corrections. She didn't change anything that she had done. She was fired. So, she didn't care. Screw the author! Her final act of defiance. So much for any control an author has over the work he (or she) created. When the book was picked up by *Simon & Schuster* several years later I hoped they would do a re-do. But, nope... What's done is done.

That's what it's like to be published...

In any case, I still get my royalty checks. Big ones, just like the one I got today. ...Though that one was actually from a different publishing for a different book...

Should I cash it or just throw it away? Hmmm, I don't know??? ☺

Have Your Earned the Right?
03/05/16 07:59

It is a very simple equation; your life is defined by what you have accomplished.

It is also a very simple equation; your life should not defined by what your think, feel, or the judgments you cast.

Many people in this world, especially in the civilized world, where free speech is a promise, believe that they can say anything they want about any-thing or any-person. But, what gives them the right? Do they possess the knowledge-base, have they gone to school and done their academic research on the subject, and/or do they possess the awarded credentials to cast judgment? Some do, but most do not. Yet, we live in a time where judgment, not conscious understanding, reigns supreme.

As one of the first-generation practitioners of the martial arts, here in the United States, who trained directly under the guidance of Asian born instructors, I would so commonly hear how many of my peers did not feel worthy to carry the torch and go off and start their own school of self-defense. There is a certain mythical quality about training under the direction of an Asian born teacher who has spent their whole life in-training. And, what the true martial arts teaches one is humility. So, from that perspective the way these advanced martial artists felt was a mindful understanding of their own respectful limitations. But, what many do not understand is that in Asian many people cast that same level of implied auspiciousness onto westerners; not earner or deserved but none-the-less it is there. This being stated, some of the aforementioned western martial art practitioners where, in fact, better proponents of the martial arts than their Asian born instructors. Yet, they held onto their belief keeping them from excelling in the craft where they had earned all of the credentials and the rights to spread their knowledge to the world. This leads us to the quandary…

We live in a world of precepts based upon beliefs held only in our own minds. Those who have studied, those who have been trained, and those who have learned at the hands of the masters are generally the one's where their egos are held in check as they know what true good and true truth looks like. On the other hand, there are many, due to having lived a life of plenty, who have nothing better to do with their time than to hold onto the misnomer that their belief is the truth and by stating their belief it will thereby be embraced by the world. They do this before having gained any foundational wisdom on which to base their conclusions. And, this is a big problem. Most people never study the in depth nature of the subject they are speaking about. They never truly study themselves with enough inner-reflection. They never study the psychology of the human being to the degree that they come to understand that a personal truth is not the truth, it is only a personal belief and should only be seen as such. They possess no level of humbleness or humility.

Just because you have a loud mouth does not mean you have anything worth saying.

Through the technology of this modern world many people are given a voice. …Many people that would never have had a voice in times gone past. And, this is a good thing. But, there are those who misuse this voice. They lead people down a dark road guided only by their ego and their own personal belief that what they believe should be believed by all — what they have to teach should be heard by all. This is dangerous and it is damaging.

If you have done the work to train and have been chosen to play on a sport's teams, you have been chosen to be a member of that team. From that point forward, you must continue to excel and refine your skills or you will be cut from the team. This is the same in the world of academia, in business, in teaching, and the list goes on. But, these are concrete entities that have been formulated with an intended goal in mind. They are formed and focused. They are not simply something someone has created in their own mind and called themselves a member or a master of.

Have you earned the right to be the voice? Yes, anyone can say anything if you live in a free society. But, is what you are saying helping or hurting? Is what you are saying making the lives of those you speak about better or worse? Is what you are speaking about helping the greater good or is it simply a way for you to expand your ego, shielding yourself from the pain, anger, or dissatisfaction you feel in that deep space inside of yourself that no one else knows about but you?

Casting judgement, looking outside of yourself is a way for you to hide from yourself and not study who you truly are and why you are feeling the things that you are feeling.

If you speak only to hide from your true inner-self or to fulfill something that is missing from your life, then who are you helping and who are you hurting? The answer: you are hurting you because you are not looking deeply enough into your own inner motivations and you are hurting whomever and/or whatever you are casting your opinions about because what you are stating is not based in elemental truth, only conjecture.

Think about it… Is what you are saying designed to help the greater good or is it simply designed to make you look good? If it is the ladder, do you think that there is no karma attached to unleashing beliefs as opposed to established facts to the world?

If you want a better life, if you want this to be a better world, it begins with what you think and what you say based upon what you think. Meaning, the first order of business is, you must refine your own mind.

You are not a teacher until you have been certified to be a teacher. Then, like the aforementioned martial artists, you should be so humble to not even consider yourself worthy to be a teacher. From this, a better, more whole society is born as you have become a more humble individual.

The greater good always begins with one person.

* * *

02/05/16 07:36

If somebody doesn't care, there is probably nothing you can do to make them care.

You Can't Make Paper from Words Written on the Internet
02/05/16 07:33

I have this friend who makes paper. It is a very cool process where she takes old paper from various sources, grinds it up to mulch in a blender, adds wherever secret ingredients, flowers, cotton, or whatever, and then paints in onto palates and lets it dry. It emerges as these very beautiful artistic pages; each unique in its own way.

As she begins the process of the grinding the old paper, I often watch and think how, here are all these words; words that someone else read, somewhere along the way. I wonder if those words helped the person who read them, inspired them, made them think; made them sad, happy, or invigorated. But, whatever the case, those words came from the creative mind of some person and were case to paper. Now, those words are washed from the hands of time only to reemerge as new forms of paper where someone else can cast their thoughts and their art. Art upon art, the perfect equation.

All this is a perfect process, I believe. Created in the mind, cast to the pages, reimagined, and then reemerged as a new source of and for art. Perfect…

The internet is not like that. It is cold, uncaring, abstract, and lost. Words are written there/here but not words cast upon the perfection of pages; simply words cast in type fonts by those hiding from who they truly are.

*   *   *

01/05/16 08:22

Words of wisdom are generally spoken by the fool.

Youth, Age, Rage,
and What To Do Between Now and Then
01/05/16 08:17

I was sitting outside at my local *Starbucks,* having a latte' in the afternoon, a few days ago. All was peaceful and well with the world. This young guy, maybe thirteen, pulls up on his skateboard. There are stairs leading to the parking lot over by one corner of the outdoor patio at Starbucks. He takes this small sound unit from his pocket. He sets it down on the stairs, turns it on — it is very-very loud with very good sound quality. I was really surprised how good it sounded for being so small. Hip-hop music blasted as he began to skate around in an area where skating is prohibited.

There is this old guy who frequents this *Starbucks;* Chinese via Australia, I believe. He is kind of like the unofficial warden of the place. Whenever any of the young guys from the nearby high school show up and light up a cigarette, he always forcefully reminds them that Starbucks is a nonsmoking environment, that they are invading the space of other people, and to put it out.

The skateboarder's music was blasting. The old guy was getting very annoyed. He tells him to turn it off and stop skating. The kid ignored him.

This all made me think back to my youth. When I had my first car when I was in high school I am sure I played *Jimi Hendrix* and *Black Sabbath* way too loud out of my 8-Track player. So much so that I am sure it annoyed a lot of people. But, that's youth in the age of rock n' roll. That's what you do.

…Side note: With the nostalgia craze of music on vinyl and cassettes in full swing, I have often wondered why no one has relaunched 8-Track tapes? I still have a functioning 8-Track player hooked up to one of my stereos. ☺ But, anyway…

The old guy was pissed. But, I am sure in his time he did a few things unsavory to the aged.

Think about it; the young always look down on the old. The old always criticize and have no respect for the young — they have seemingly forgotten what it means to be young. But, it is so short of a distance between one and the other and all we have is the time in between.

The Test of Time
30/04/16 06:59

What you do today, what you say today, how you behave today directly affects what you will experience tomorrow. What you do tomorrow, what you say tomorrow, how you behave tomorrow directly affects what you will experience the day after tomorrow.

What are you doing, saying, and how are you behaving?

Life is a process created by your interactions with those around you. How you interact not only defines who you are as a person but it comes to detail how you are perceived and, thus, what opportunities will be presented to you in the future. Your actions create your reality. Your actions create your tomorrow.

Most people do not think about the bigger-reality. They do not think or even care about what they put out the world. In this age of cyberspace there is a cloak between the self and reality. Not seen, you are safe. But, are you?

What you have done is what you have done. What you have said is what you have said. How you have behaved is how you have behaved and even if no one knows that it is you who has done or said these things it *is* you who has done and said these thing. Thus, it is you who has defined the next stage of your existence.

As the martial arts are obviously a big part of my life, I often reference stories encountered during my years of involvement. Let me indulge again... I know I have told this story before somewhere, but it goes to the point... Maybe twenty years ago when my first book on Hapkido had just been published, I was contacted, via email, by some guy who didn't like the book and/or me. It was a point in internet history when cross platform email was fairly new and I foolishly believed that I was required to answer any email sent my direction.

As stated, the guy didn't like the book or me. His attacks were so adolescent that I initially assumed that he was a teenage but as it went back and forth a few times, with me playing nice, it turned out that he was an actual school owner. Perhaps the funniest thing of the discourse, and his biggest compliant, was that he didn't like that I had my name and my rank on my belt. He said that was not hapkido and he sent me a copy of pictures from a 1960s Black Belt Magazine where the man the article was about had nothing on his belt. So, that must be the law of the land. Well, that was the 1960s not the 1990s… The joke was, the man in the article was one of my instructors. I eventually suggested that if the guy didn't like my book to write his own and find a publisher. He assured me he would and he'd show me. Of course, that never happened. He simply wanted to spend his time venting at me via email. Proving what, I do not know? I don't even remember his name.

You see, there is a small subset of marital artists who really approach life from an insecure mindset. I am better. My instructor is better. My style is better. The way I practice the style is better. And, you are not as good.

Anyone who comes at life from this mindset is destine for a confrontationally based existence and for failure.

The fact is, this is not just in the martial arts. Think how many people interact with life via this same pattern. They know more, are more, should be more, and are better than you. Wrong!

As a journalist, I wrote for this one martial arts magazine for over a decade. It is not that I had any desire to do so, but I knew the editor and he knew that I had the ability to get an article done extremely rapidly; the same day if it came down to crunch time. So, he continually gave me assignments. And, we all have to pay our rent, so, I wrote…

Most of the people I interviewed were truly good individuals, simply attempting to give back to the world via the martial arts. Every now and then, however, I would have to speak with someone that was so full of themselves it was simply scary. They were this, they were that. They were going to do this; they were going to do that. All about how great they were, how great their school was, and how they were the greatest example of the martial arts and were climbing the ladder of success to the top. They were this while everyone else was less. When I spoke with them, I just wanted to scream. When I had to write the article, I wanted to scream louder. But, I just did the job and got it done. But, where are those people now? I don't know? Their schools are gone and they have fallen off of the map just like the guy who contacted me about my book all of those years ago.

If you come at life as a knower, you better know. If you attack and criticize other people, you better already be more than they will ever be. If your only contribution to life is telling everyone how great you are or how lowly another person is; when the truth get told through time, who is going to be left to believe you?

And, this is the point. ...Will what you are doing, what you are saying, how you are behaving stand the test of time? Will what you do or say achieve anything for your tomorrow? And, more importantly, will what you are doing today help the future; not just your future but everyone's?

Life is based upon interactions. How you interact is how you will be judged. Are your interactions leading to a better you and a greater good or are they simply leading to a greater you, (only in your own mind) — a greater you that, at best, will only last for this moment?

There are feeble minded people who will believe anything anyone says. But, if they believe your lies of today, they will believe someone else's lies of tomorrow. As your words and your friendships are not set in stone, what guarantees do you have of someone's/anyone's belief in you lasting any longer than while they are enamored by your words or persona?

You may love someone; you may hate someone. You may love something; you may hate something. First of all, those emotions are based in you and emanate from you. That means they are only believed by you. But, more than that, it is your reaction to your emotions which guides how you will pass through your life.

What you do today, what you say today, how you behave today directly affects what you will experience tomorrow. What you do tomorrow, what you say tomorrow, how you behave tomorrow directly affects what you will experience the day after tomorrow.

What are you doing, saying, and how are you going to behave?

* * *

30/04/16 06:38

Who you were yesterday does not have to be the definition of who you are today. You have the potential to change if you truly want to. But, people will remember who you used to be. How do you change the perception in their mind?

Who Do You Owe What?
29/04/16 07:16

I believe that for each of us someone comes into our lives and they really help us to become. …Become more. …Become more of who we want to be and who we were destine to be.

But, it is essential to note that becoming more is a choice. People who posses the skills, people who can teach us, people who we can truly learn from come into the lives of all of us at various points throughout all of our lifetimes. Yet, how many people actually, *"Become?"* Very few, I think.

Each person is defined by their own set of parameters; their own set of definitions: psychological and otherwise. Each person is who they are. Though most people do wish to, "Become," not all possess the drive or the skillset to take what they have learned and move out and forward on their own to achieve it.

Commonly, I have found that those who do not possess this drive feel very dissatisfied with their life. They are often envious of those who have taken what they have learned and have stepped into their own limelight. None-the-less, these people were also presented with the steps to make their dreams a reality, yet they could not or did not move into their own sense of becoming.

This is an important thing to think about as you move through life. What are you doing to become who you want to be? If someone comes into your life who has a skillset that you wish to learn about, do you have the capacity to learn? Do you treat them as a true teacher and actually take what they have given you and formulate it to guide you on the road to your own achievement or do you find an excuse to step away from them and/or not personally put into practice what they have taught you?

There are a million people who have achieved things in their life. But, there are a billion who have not. Which one are you?

The teachers are out there. For the most part those who have the skills are happy to pass them along. But, do you seek those people out? Do you learn from them? Then, do you take what you have learned and make it your own, creating your own whatever?

This is your life. You are not whole and total onto yourself, until you have become the ideal expression of yourself.

Learn, accomplish, and then teach. This is the lifestyle of those who have become who they were destine to become.

Do you ever watch the doing get done?
28/04/16 08:03

I live above this golf course. Though I don't play golf I sometimes watch the goings-on down below. I observe as the golfers practice and practice upon the putting green, attempting to make their shot perfect. I watch as the gardeners trim the law and the trees attempting to design them into the shape that is locked in its own artistic perfection while giving the masses what they want.

Life is all about the doing. It is about how you do what you do. Some people don't care, they do the most half-assed job in anything that they attempt, and whatever they do always comes out being a mess. Others are so focused that it takes them forever to do anything. But, is what they accomplish ever the perfection that they seek in their mind?

Certainly, in the tradition(s) born of Zen Buddhism there is an enormous amount of focus put on how the doing gets done. This mindset translated into the martial arts which lead to the enormous amount of focus the practitioner puts on the, *"Getting it right."* They practice their techniques over-and-over again attempting to find meditative perfection in their physical movements.

But, at the end of the day, each person is just what each person is. They can do what they can do only as good as they can do. Through practice each of us can become better. But, most of us never practice at anything — we don't try to become better. We are just here, we do what we do, and then we are gone leaving nothing worth leaving.

If perfecting the process is the key to the making things as right as they can be, then process has to be the tool that we each use to make the, *"Us,"* and the, *"Whatever we do,"* the best as it can be.

What is your process?

People in Their Present
28/04/16 07:22

Have you ever watched someone become very amped up about a subject? Have you ever watched them go into a rage screaming their ideologies to the world? Have you ever watched them rant and rave and then you realize what they are talking about does not even affect their life in any way, shape, or form? Have you ever done this? Have you ever caused yourself to become enraged about another person or another situation that does not affect your life in any manner? Have you ever asked yourself, *"Why?"*

It is easy to find a subject to obsess about. It is easy to try to present yourself as an authority on that subject to the ears of someone who does not know the facts. Again, the question goes to, *"Why?"* Why do you waste your life time and your life energy on something that does not affect who you truly are?

You only have the time to obsess about something when you have noting better to do.

People look for a distraction from the reality of their own dismal life. Those who are the most vocal about the things that do not truly affect them are commonly the ones with, *"Dismal,"* raining down upon them. They are unhappy with their own existence, they are unfulfilled in their own existence, thus, they look for something to focus on outside of themselves and their dismal life. This has been the case forever… First there were stories told around the campfire, then books, then plays, then newspapers and magazines, then movies, and now the internet. But, wherever and whatever it is, it is, *"Out there,"* it is not, *"In here."*

"In here," is a very hard place for many people, as they do not want to look at themselves — as they do not wish to study their own inner workings and what they can do to make their own self and their own life more; they do not want to look at the creative process that lead them to the state

they are currently in. Thus, instead, they focus on the, *"Out there."*

"Out there" is much easier than, *"In here." "Out there,"* takes no effort. *"Out there,"* takes no discipline.

Life is a process. For some, life is easier than for others. For some, life is happier than for others. For some, life is more embellished than for others. But, the fact remains, if you want anything to change in your life, if you want to be better, happier, more content, more fulfilled you have to focus on yourself not on some other person that you have never met and never will met or upon some abstract ideology that you will never posses all of the fact about.

You want your life to feel better, stop focusing on the, *"Out there."* Instead, focus on the, *"In here."*

* * *

27/04/16 14:09

Why does it matter to you?

* * *
27/04/16 12:09

If a person hides who they truly are, that deception should be seen as the defining factor of their life.

* * *

27/04/16 12:07

If you think that saying something bad equals something good you're wrong.

* * *

27/04/16 07:39

If you're looking for something to be negative about, you can find it.

If you're looking for something to be positive about, you can find it.

Spare Any Change?
27/04/16 07:23

I'm directing this new music video and I was on my way over to *Sunset Gower Studios* where the sound stage for the shoot is located. En route I decided to stop by *The Original Farmer's Market* and grab my favorite L.A. breakfast; a Number Twenty-Three (23) at *The French Crepe Company,* which is basically a Belgium waffle with fresh strawberries, butter, syrupy, and lots of whip crème, which you self-apply. I love whip crème! And, a latte; non-fat, of course.

I was sitting at a table. They had served up my latte' so I was kicking back, sipping it, and enjoying the sites and the sounds as I awaited my waffle. A young Korean man walks up to me and asks if I can, *"Spare any change?"* First of all, this type of occurrence is very unusual at Farmer's Market. In fact, it's pretty much unheard of. Security is very tight. Ever since the no smoking and the paparazzi craze hit. ...Now, the roaming security guard really watch over the place. So, people who are asking for money, or doing anything else sketchy, are really never seen.

In any case, he was a young guy, maybe eighteen, nineteen, or so. I could tell he hadn't been on the low for too long as his clothes looked just a few days deep. You could see he was strung out thought. If you've been around, you develop an eye for that kind of things. So, I knew what he wanted the money for. I declined...

Previously, I had noticed that there were two Korean women sitting at a table not far from mine. One saw the guy as he was asking for money, stood up and walked over, as he was walking away. Speaking to him in Korean she asked if he wanted something to eat. He accepted. She ordered him whatever he wanted from the menu at The French Crepe Company. She paid. Then, her and her friend got their stuff together and left. The guy stood there for a few moments and then he too turned and walked away. A few minutes later I watched as the counter clerk called out the number for him to pick up his meal but he was long gone. They called it out several times until they finally took it back behind the counter and probably threw it away.

The moral of the story... I don't really know? I do know that drugs are a bad thing. I have known more than a few people who have died from their ingestion. Drugs lead you down a bad road. No matter what drug it is, that drug does have its consequences.

The lady, her heart was in the right place. She did the right thing. She offered the guy some food. The guy, I guess he just didn't care about food. His mind was on obtaining something else — focused on getting another type of nutrition. So, he walked on looking for a means to get it.

Have you ever watched a junky get their fix: be it junk, crack, coke, even weed? They fall back into a trance of satisfaction. But, it is not naturally induced. They need something to get them there. And, look where that road to getting that, *"Something,"* leads.

What do you need to get you into your trance of satisfaction? What is the price today? And, what will be the price tomorrow?

* * *

26/04/16 13:45

Is your truth the real truth or is it only a lie that you created in your own mind?

* * *

26/04/16 13:43

Do you believe the lie?

Yoga: Union with God
26/04/16 07:49

Many people do not know this fact but the word, *"Yoga,"* actually means, *"Union,"* or *"Yoking,"* with god. To most, yoga is simply a term that describes the physical postures that helps one with flexibility, health, and now, through the various methods of physical exercise, performed in a very-heated environment, to lose weight.

The style of yoga that involves the physical postures is actually termed, *"Hatha Yoga."* Though Hatha Yoga is an elemental part of the overall sphere of the yoga experience, its practice is primarily limited to the physical postures, with a bit of breath control on the side. The belief is, Hatha Yoga will unite the body with the mind and thereby guide one towards the gates of god realizations.

Remember the entire purpose of all forms of yoga is to cause one to come into communion with the divine. It is not simply a method to lose weight.

Last Thanksgiving, I was drinking some nice wine with my extended family who are all Korean. Two of my female cousins-in-law where discussing their yoga classes. I brought up the subject about what yoga truly means. They joking dismissed me and finding out that I had written books on yoga… (My book on pranayama is apparently used as a teaching tool for several yoga schools. Thanks!) …they asked me to do some postures. But, believe me when I tell you, long term martial arts training destroys the joints. So, standing on my head in full lotus posture, like I used to be able to do, is no longer an option but I do have a photograph. ☺ But, I am getting off point…

Koreans are a very religious culture. They are a very Christian culture. Virtually all of my relatives are ardent church-goers. The thing is, the concept of god in Hinduism, where yoga was born, is quite different from the god of Christianity. For this reason, forever, I have seen it taught in

Christian communities that things like yoga and meditation are bad as by doing these things you allow a pathway for the devil to enter. I, of course, don't believe that. But...

In the late sixties and through the mid seventies, Yoga was everywhere. Yoga classes were everywhere. I used to teach them. Now, like then, Yoga is everywhere. I think more now than then because there are tons of self-standing yoga schools that exist. Then, not like now, everyone understood it was a spiritually based practice. Now, everyone just uses these weird concoctions that are calling yoga as a way to lose weight. No one knows and/or no longer even cares that yoga is supposed to be a spiritual practice that unites the practitioner with god. The perfect example of marketing to the masses...

I don't know, is the world getting better or worse?

* * *

26/04/16 07:22

If you give into the demands of another person, they will always demand something more.

Do Something Nice
25/04/16 08:08

I often speak about how people get very amped-up and are adrenalized when they are involved with something that makes them angry. But, why are you angry? This question is especially important to ask yourself when you are angry about something that does not even really concern you. Why do you focus your thoughts on someone or something that has nothing to do with your day-to-day existence? Is your life so empty that you need to look outside of yourself for life validating emotion-generating experiences?

As I also often discuss, this anger-based mindset can be very addicting. Once it is experienced, there is a certain type of person that seeks it out over-and-over again. Some feel it is their calling to unleash their anger based opinions and ideologies to the world. But, all negativity does does is make the world a much more pain-driven place. It never makes anything better.

Let's switch all of this up: right here, right now. Stop it! Stop embracing anger. Stop embracing negativity. Go and do something nice.

Tweeted and Deleted
24/04/16 07:47

Have you ever said something that you wish you hadn't said? Have you ever said something that you wish you could take back? I believe that most of us have.

Have you ever heard something somebody else said about you that you didn't like? Have you ever wished those words could be removed from the minds of the masses? I believe that most of us have.

If you have a conscience and you say something wrong... ...Sometime things come out in a way that you didn't really mean... In those cases, when we are face-to-face, most of us try to rectify our statement. This is especially the case if you are affected by your words in association with whom you said them about. I mean, you don't want to piss off your friends, teachers, coworkers, or family... We don't want to seem crass, mean, or uncaring so we say something else to make it better or apologize for our misspoken statement.

This is the case if you care about someone. What about if you don't care about them? In those cases, are you willing to apologize, are you willing to respeak your words or remove them? Probably not.

Many people live their lives from a very selfish state of consciousness. Most people, (you included), do not even care until what you say or what you do affects you in some negative manner. Why is that?

Many people live their lives from a state of consciousness where they are happy to lash out and hurt other people, release their misplaced aggressions as a process of venting to make themselves feel somehow better. They are happy to do this until they are hurt by someone else. Then, they become all aghast. Why is that? I mean, what should they expect?

As a church-going Christian friend of mine once told me many years ago, *"The internet is the devil's tool."* So said her minister. When you think of it from that perspective, it is true. It is the *"One-nation,"* spoken of in *The Book of Revelations.* It is a place where people speak, hide, hurt, and deceive with little or no consequence. Do you participate?

As in all cases, the question goes to you. Who are you and what do you do while on this devil's tool? Do you speak with no boundaries; experiencing no consequences? Do you feed the falsity of your beliefs and your ego to the world? Do you take or hurt and then hide? Or, do you do something good? Maybe even fixing what you said wrong?

Do you tweet and delete?

*   *   *

24/04/16 07:07

You can't threaten someone with excommunication if they don't care about being a member of the group, just as you can't threaten someone with impeding breakup if they no longer want to be in the relationship.

Swamji and Me
23/04/16 09:52

As you may or may not know, I am a bit of a bibliophile. I collect books. My main quest is for rare Eastern Metaphysical and spiritually based writings. In any case, I came upon a book being offered online created around photographs of my teacher, Swami Satchidananda, titled, *Sri Swami Satchidananda: Portrait of a Modern Sage*. I was drawn to the book for two reasons, it was signed and it was a hardcover copy which is apparently hard to come by. So, it was bit pricy, but whatever, I bought it. The fact is, I never even knew about this book. It was published in 1996 but I guess I just never came across a copy.

In any case, I ordered it and it arrived. I unpack it and I opened it up to a random page. Damn, there I am! A photograph with me, the L.A. crew, and Gurudev on page 135. I was both extremely happy and shocked. I obviously knew about this photograph and I clearly remember the day it was taken. But, wow, what a flood of memories.

Swami Satchidananda and his teachings were a very essential part of my adolescent years, early adult years, and my spiritual upbringing. I have written about experiences I had with him in various other places, most notably in the book, *Zen: Tales from the Journey*. But, to be cast back like this, it was quite a happy shock.

Above that photograph is another photograph where it is the back of the disciple's heads, as Gurudev was in the foreground. My head is there too. But, you'd only know it if you knew what the back of my long blonde haired head looked like back then. ☺ That photo was taken during one of the very intimate satsangs we would have with him on Saturday nights at the ashram in Santa Barbara when he was in town.

I was Swami Satchidananda's soundman for a number of years. Back then, spirituality was very high on the minds of the masses. (Not now). So, he used to give a lot of lectures. I would pack my equipment up in my '76 Dodge van and travel to, set up, and recorder the words he spoke. Man, so many memories from those experiences… He was a wise teacher. At these small satsangs, however, he didn't need a mic. I did record some of them for posterity but not all. Obviously, the one portrayed in the photograph, I did not.

I really think if you truly hope to learn anything from a teacher you need to develop a personal relationship with them. You really need to be close enough to them to come to understand who they truly are. From this, you gain the complex understanding of what it takes to be a good human being, while remaining centered on spirituality. Too many people, I believe, cast their faith to those that are unmeetable as they are no longer in their human body. From this, myth is born. Is myth the truth? Usually not.

A couple of pages deeper in the book, page 138, if you look really hard you can see me again in and amongst the disciples. It was outside on a rainy day and it was the inauguration of the Santa Barbara ashram. My face is partially blocked by another disciple but my IYI (integral Yoga Institute) friend Hari is behind me, Uma is a bit in front. Shiva was in the photo as was Sister Maji, Jadhana, and the list goes on. The funny thing is, at least to me, is that in the photograph all eyes are on Gurudev but I was obviously saying something to the girl I had brought with me, Carol. A girl who I had met at the Sufi Dances and was totally infatuated with at the time. I though if there was a woman worth giving up bramacharya for, she was it. ☺ I joked to a person I showed the book to, *"All eyes were on the guru but my eyes were on the girl."* That's funny now but back then I was seriously devolved to the formal spiritual lifestyle. If you feel like it, you can read a story about that day, and my interaction with that girl and the spiritual group, also in the book, *Zen: Tales from the Journey.*

Those were good and important times for me…

The last time I actually interacted with Gurudev was when I was twenty-four. By this point I had fallen away from the IYI as I felt the people in control of the group had become a little bit too full of themselves. I had gone to India, did what I did there, had returned and was going to grad school. It had been a few years but, out of the blue, I received a call from Padma asking me if I would/could do the sound for a lecture Gurudev was giving. I accepted.

I got the equipment together, brought my beautiful Spanish via Cuba girlfriend with me, (yes, I had left bramacharya behind), and it was an overall great experience. It had been a few years since I had seen Gurudev by that point and he kept joking, *"Who's this, who's this,"* in regard to me. The day went as the day went. I never saw him in person again.

It was a great memory churner to discover this book. I am sure that there are a lot of other photographs out there of me in association with Gurudev – photographs I will probably never see. Me, I never carried a camera back then... But, the memories are there.

From my point of view, most people just pass through their life, grabbing at whatever they can to keep themselves in a state of unsecured momentary happiness. They move from one thing to the next, one desire to the next, attempting to hold on to something that they cannot define. Few people attempt to find deeper meaning. I think that is sad. I believe that you must first know yourself, then study yourself, removing as many obstacles and bad qualities from yourself as possible, and then move forward into the greater MORE. How you do this, is your choice. For me, at least in my early years, it was defined by Swami Satchidanada and the Sufi Order.

Life is a funny thing. But, if we do not attempt to make ourselves more and better and do good things for other people, what does it all mean?

Do You Care About Me?
22/04/16 20:31

In life, you can only care about someone else when your life is not on the line. You can only care about someone else when you have the time to think, feel, imagine, and dream. You can only care about someone when you possess the ability to know how to love.

People speak about caring about someone else all the time. But, who are these people? And, do they really care?

Life is made up of a complex set of human interactions. When someone, *"Cares,"* about someone else do they really care or do they simply care about what that person can give them: be it love, lust, money, companionship, knowledge, you name it? Is their caring true caring or is their caring based upon some hidden agenda — a hidden agenda that the individual who claims to care may not even realize that they have?

Have you ever had to fight for your life to survive? In those situations, there is no time to care for someone else. Your entire life experience is brought into the absolute now of the moment and survival is all that can be front and center to your mind. A fight, a war, drowning, starvation, a plane crash, a car accident, all of these things and more bring an individual to absolute now consciousness. Who do you care about when you don't have time to even think about caring?

Caring only takes place when you have the time and the presence of mind to care. Some people are very selfish, they never truly care for or about anyone. Others, do care. They want a person or an entire people to be safe, happy, and fulfilled. But, just because they care does not mean that the caring is returned. Have you ever cared about someone, did something for them, and they returned your gesture with dismissal, indignity, or injustice? Did you still care for them after that innocent occurred?

Take a moment. Think about who you care about. Think about why you care about them. Really get to the bottom of your emotion. Ask yourself, *"Would you care about them if they didn't care about you?"*

How many people have passed through your life and at one point you felt all kinds of emotions towards them — you really cared about them. Now, they are gone. How to you feel about them at this point in your life?

Caring is a choice. It is a good choice. It is better to care than to desire to injure someone. For anyone you injure, in any way, shape, or form, so too will you be injured. That is the simple truth of life.

You do not have the right to pass judgment on anyone for any reason but what you do have the right to do is to care. If you care, you care. Caring is forever good but you have to understand the source of your caring. You have to care even if they don't know you care. You have to care even if they don't care about you. That is true caring.

To many people caring is only a condition locked in their mind. They think about someone, wish them well, hope the best for them, even pray for them but all this is all just mind-stuff. It is not true caring. True caring is doing something positive in this physical world for a person. True caring is taking action to make another person's mind, body, and life better.

Who do you are about? What does your caring mean? What does your caring equal? What are you going to do for them because you care about them?

That's Just What They Do
22/04/16 09:39

Where I live I have an exceptional view of the Pacific Ocean. I am always so awe inspired and thankful whenever I look out of my windows.

This morning I was standing on my patio with a cup of coffee and there was a group of about twelve birds flying, hovering, and interacting right in front of me. They flew this way and that, came back around, and just did what they did; flying. Nothing to accomplish, nothing else better to do. It was beautiful.

The thing about most peace-based animals and fowl is that they simply exist. They exist doing what they're doing with no thought to be doing something/anything else. We human beings are not like that, however. It is all about the advancement, the power-play, the being, the becoming, the I am that and you are not — all about the ownership and the competition.

Sad I think… How much of our life is wasted in the mind of no peace, no suchness, no anything but greed and desire that leads to all of the negative emotion like anger and lust that then leads to all of the hurtful actions that humans unleash.

We should all try to become nicer and freer.

What is he talking about?
22/04/16 08:52

Have you ever been forced into a conversation with a person and you can't help but ask yourself, *"What is he talking about?"* You don't like what the person is saying, you don't agree with what that person is saying, you think what they are saying is stupid, or maybe you don't even understand what they are talking about or why? In these incidences you have the option to turn and walk away, stand there listening while hating life, boiling on the inside but smiling on the outside, or you can confront them and tell them to shut up. Your choice is most probably based upon your personality. But, none of the choices are really a good one.

We've all been in these situations. Mostly, with people we've just met but sometimes with people we've known for a long time.

Some people think some very ridiculous things based upon who knows what? But, what can we do? That's just life.

Some people simply avoid people so they will not be lead into this style of dialogue. But, that doesn't always work. They're out there and they're going to find you.

The thing you have to think about is, has anyone ever felt that way about you? Have you ever been in a conversation, speaking your mind, and was the person you were talking to screaming on the inside because of what you were saying but not reacting? Where they hating every moment of life that they were being forced to listen to you but they kept a smile on their face while you kept talking?

Most people don't think about this. They form their opinions in their mind, surround themselves with those of like-mind, and never care or think about what they are spewing into the world and the effect it is having on others.

Everybody is different. Everybody thinks what they think. Everybody wants to be heard. But, the truth be told, the only one's who actually care what you have to say are the people who care about you (for whatever reason). And, even then they sometimes don't want to listen to what you have to say.

People use their words to get heard. Some people use their words to find validation and to prove to themselves that they actually possess a voice that is worth hearing — that they are someone and something. Some people believe that they need to be heard, thus they speak, never talking into consideration if the person or person's they are talking to even wants to hear what they have to say.

Before you speak, think who you are speaking to. Question, do they want to hear what you have to say? If you don't do this all the time, your words do nothing but ruin the space of perfect silence and inner-calm that would exist in this world if you had said nothing.

RIP
21/04/16 14:25

Sadly, Prince passed away today. It is really pretty scary how many seminal figures in music are gone this year and it's only April. I mean Bowie, Glen Frey, Paul Kantner, Merle Haggard, Maurice White, Natalie Cole (who passed away on December 31st but most of us heard about it on the 1st), and even the Prince protégé Vanity; gone…

It hasn't been released yet what caused Prince to die at such a young age… Fifty-seven, (the same age as me and I feel so young). But, I was listening to Steve Jones on *Jonesy's Jukebox* today; Lenny Kravitz was his guest. They both implied that they know. CNN just stated that the Minneapolis coroner is going to do an autopsy. So, I guess it will eventually be revealed. But, whatever the cause, it is a big loss.

I always respected Prince and how he stood up for the Intellectual Property Rights of an artist to own and control the rights to their work and have jurisdiction over the way in which their creations were used by other people. He was one of the first big star to go up against the record companies and actually win, though it did take many years. And, he was one of the first artists to help reshape the laws in regard to the way people could use an artist's creations without the appropriate consent and payment. But, more than that, think about the amount of great music he created. How many songs he recorded that are just so memorable. He really influenced a lot of people and his music will continue to do so.

The world has truly lost a great contributor to modern culture.

* * *

21/04/16 08:35

Never believe anything at face value as there is always a deeper story to be known.

Eviction
21/04/16 07:46

Last night, on the news, I was watching a story about how this family was being evicted from the apartment they had lived in for almost twenty years in Boyle Heights. The landlord's attorney claimed the reason for the eviction was that the couple had two additional children since they moved into the apartment that were not listed on the original rental agreement. The couple claims there never was an original rental agreement and the new landlord was simply evicting them because they were under Rent Control and the landlord wants to raise the rent and make more money which can only happen if he moves-in new tenants.

There was a protest launched to help the family. There were a lot of people taking part in the protest in this predominately Latino section of L.A. There was even a bunch of young, bearded, white hipster with nothing better to do.

Near the end of the story they reveal the building. It was unexpected. It was an old, square, rundown brick building; really junky. It immediately made me flashback to my childhood.

In 1969, when I was eleven years old, my mother and I moved from our apartment about a block off of Hollywood Boulevard to a building that looked very similar to the building in the news story. It was a junky old hotel on the corner of Normandy and 6th Street. My mother had apparently lived there for a time when she arrived in L.A. a couple of decades before and she remembered it as being fairly nice. Maybe back then... By the time I was there it was old rundown and inhabited by a bunch of lonely senior citizens with no place left to go awaiting their death.

Moving probably wasn't all that bad of thing for me. I mean, I had already dropped acid by that point in my life with some of the hippies I used to hang out with at *Barnsdall*

Park. What they were thinking giving a kid acid? I don't know? But, it was the sixties.

Anyway, the time I lived there, throughout the 6th grade, was a fairly unhappy time for me. There were cockroaches on the wall, the water for taking a bath was rarely warm enough, the people were all so fucking old, and life pretty much sucked. Yet, there I was…

The building has remained in place for all of these years. A couple of weeks ago I happened to drive by it and, low-and-behold, it has now become a boutique hotel. I looked it up on Yelp and it has a really high rating. I didn't know whether to laugh or to cry, it was such a weird emotion. When I lived there it was a dump, now it is a sought after place to be. Sometimes I just don't get life ???

But, back to the initial story of this story… There they are, this family fighting to stay in their apartment. …The dumpy, rundown place that they call home. The landlord only thinking about his bank account. Who knows, maybe he wants to evict all the tenants and make the building into a boutique hotel?

Everybody Wants to Fight but Nobody Knows How to Fight
21/04/16 07:44

I forever find it very curious how people in this world are so confrontational. I find this particularly interesting in a place like the United States where people are so on the edge of anger for absolutely no reason at all.

Have you ever been in the middle of war zone? Have you ever been in the middle of a riot? Have you ever been attacked by a gang of thugs? In those situations, there you have a reason to be confrontational – for in those situations it is kill or be killed. But, in the modern civilized world we live in a place where peace and prosperity abound. Yet, people are dominated by their anger, leading to confrontation(s). Why is this?

To provide a couple of examples. I was driving down the street today, a guy was at the stop sign in front of me, playing with his phone or something. When he didn't drive on when the traffic was clear I gave him a little honk to wake him up to the fact that there are other people in the world. He dove on but was giving me dirty looks like he wanted to fight. He was a late middle aged man with a handicap plaque handing on his mirror. But, he wanted to fight. I laughed at him.

Yesterday, I was driving along and was about to change lanes. I put on my turn signal. As I did the car behind me immediately raced into the lane to intentionally cut me off. My initial thought was this was one of those people who try to get into accidents so they can collect insurance money. But, I responded quickly and stayed my course. The car pulls up next to me and it was female Latin woman, yelling and screaming at me. She wanted a fight. I smiled.

In a world of plenty, why doesn't everyone have enough? Everyone wants more. When they do not get all the ALL that they feel they deserve, they embrace anger; be it road rage or whatever. They look for a fight. But, is a fight what they really want? I don't think so.

As I often discuss, in association with the martial arts, there are those of us who train a lifetime to refine our fighting skills, solely so that we will not need to use them. Most people are not like that, however. They are not a trained fighter, yet they feel they have ability, based in anger, to go up against someone who is. Here is where many of the problems of the world begin. People enter into confrontations over their anger, when there is no reason to do so. And, in doing so, they are easily defeated.

As I always tell my students, the moment you enter into any physical altercation you must size up your opponent. As a trained fighter, you can quickly tell if the opponent you are encountering is a trained fighter or not. As I also always tell my students, the moment you realize that you are a going up against an untrained fighter, turn it down a notch. For, though you can easily beat them to a pulp, the entire reason you train in the martial arts is so you will not have to do so.

Certainly, if you are attacked you have every right to defend yourself. But, you should only fight as hard as you must fight. You should never demolish your opponent simply because you can. This is what true martial art training is all about.

Moreover, one of the main reasons one trains in the martial arts is so that they may learn mastery over their mind. From this, they will not be dominated by uncontrolled and misguided anger. Without the need to express uncontrolled, unreasonable anger, your life become so much less confrontational and free from conflict; both external and internal.

Anger, only dominates the unenlightened. Anger is the most animalistic emotion of all emotions. One who is dominated by anger exits at the lowest level of human consciousness. Yes, you may encounter people like this as you travel through your life but you do not need to allow their anger to instigate it in you. Be more than the aggressive individual(s) you encounter. If they attack you, defend yourself, but only to the necessary-end of keeping yourself free from injury. You do not have to annihilate them to win.

    Just because someone is angry at you, (for whatever reason), does not mean that you have to be angry at them. Use your martial arts training to cause you to forever raise above those dominated by anger.

* * *

20/04/16 19:51

No one wants to admit their own sins but everyone wants to call out the sins of others.

Don't you have anything better to do?
20/04/16 10:54

Every now and then someone will bring to my attention to the fact that there is discussion going on about me on the internet. Mostly, I'm doing other stuff and I really don't care so I don't check it out. Sometimes, however, if I'm just screwing around on-line when they alert me to the fact, I do take a moment and read them. Some are positive dialogues. Thanks! Others… What I always find is that the inception of the conversation was begun by a very articulate individual who is trying to cast shade on my life and me in a very subtle manner. Those make smile. The assumptions are false. The claims are misplaced. But, the writing is good. Some are just the, *"This guy is a fucking asshole!"* Those make me smile too because the person writing them does not know me at all. Like the old saying goes, *"To know me is to love me."* I think I'm a nice guy. ☺

Spending my life in the world of martial arts this type of attack is not new to me. It seems there is always some insecure practitioner attempting to create doubt about someone else. Sad but true. I have written about this phenomenon in the past…

But, it forever perplexes me why anyone discuses me at all. Don't you have anything better to do? I mean, I am just a very basic sort of guy who makes weird movies, writes books, makes music, takes some photographs, teaches a class or a seminar every now and then, and stuff like that.

…There was a filmmaking team who made a mockumentary about me maybe a decade back at *Grand Valley State University* in Michigan. I thought that was pretty funny. Zen Filmmaking !!! You can get to it from my YouTube page if you feel like it. I imagine they were doing it for a filmmaking class or something. But, at least they created something and probably earned a grade for it.

What always boggles my mind is, what does talking about and discussing another person equal? What does trying to make me or any other person look good, look bad, or look like anything equal? What does it prove and what does it do for your life — especially if you are hiding behind a screen name? Though, the truth be told, I have watched a couple of people cause their on-line notoriety to rise by discussing and/or talking trash about me (and other people). But, they never even said, *"Thank you."* ☺

As the joke goes, *"You know you can believe everything that is on the internet."* I mean any person who wants to can find a place to get their voice heard on the internet. But, why is your voice wasted talking about other people?

I remember back a number of years ago, I was watching a Run Run Shaw movie with a group of people and someone commented that his name was the same as mine. I made the joke, *"I'm half Chinese."* A couple of weeks later I was alerted to the fact that it was listed on some website that, *"Scott Shaw is half Chinese."* I mean, come on people… And, I have seen a few other pretty ridiculous things mentioned about me on the internet. But, the thing is, what can I do? This is the internet, anyone can say anything that they want: positive, negative, or just straight up bullshit. They can say it about anyone or anything.

Some of these, *"Writers,"* present their thoughts, beliefs, and accusations as though they are the truth. They are not the truth but there is a certain segment of society who believes something simply because they read it. Thus, if someone believes something, in that regard, it somehow does become the truth — at least in the mind of that individual. This is how false accusations and misguided beliefs have the potential to truly damage a person's life. And, what is the karma for that, if you are the one instigating or embellishing falsehood and hurting someone else's life? But, I guess most people who do that kind of stuff don't care.

And... I always feel thanks for the people who rise to my defense (and the defense of others) when they attempt to countermand the spreading negativity by inserting their positive opinions and/or truth based facts.

The fact is, who and what I am, what I have or have not accomplished is one hundred percent verifiable. I don't care about accolades so you are not going to find me listing mine. *"Just the facts..."* Other people may put them out there, but not me. I don't think about things like that. All I think about is what I haven't accomplished and what I've yet to accomplish. Yet, some people attempt to embellish or diminish who and what I am; what I have done. Why? I don't know. What does it prove? Some people even try to describe my life and my life motivation. But, they have never even met me, so how do they know anything about me? But, as they used to say on, *The X-Files, "The truth is out there."*

Now, all of this rambling about me brings us to the point of this blog. What are you doing with your life? Are you doing something for you? Doing something for the people you love? Accomplishing something with your life? Doing something for the greater good? Counteracting acting negativity wherever you find it? Or, are you wasting the very short amount of time that you have in LIFE obsessing about someone or something else? Attempting to either put them on a pedestal or cast them to the depths of hell?

My advice, if you love someone or something they created, support them. If you hate someone or something they created, support them, as well, because they are giving you a reason to think, study, and question life.

Ultimately, focus on your own life. Make your own life more. Then, you won't need to focus on my life or the life of any other person. You won't need to make yourself look right while attempting to make others look wrong. By accomplishing your own accomplishments, your life becomes a creative masterpiece based upon your own vision.

From this, you can stop talking about other people and start being alerted to the fact that other people are talking about you. ☺

Positive, Negative and What Is the What Is
19/04/16 16:46

In my previous blog I discussed a little bit about how some people motivate themselves into embracing and relishing negativity. But, I think we have to look at bit further into this issue and what we can do to countermand the process of spreading negativity.

As a person, I try to only allow positive people into my life. Whatever they do to make a living is unimportant to me as long as they leave a wake of positivity behind themselves. Many are working stiffs. This is life and we must do what we must do to make a living. They live their life, create their memories, and move through this process just like the rest of us.

The fact is, what you do to keep a roof over your head, as you pass through life, is not as important as how you pass through life. Are you living in a positive manner doing what you do or not? Who are you helping? Who are you hurting? Few people ask themselves this question.

The workplace is where you are forced to encounter many people of many minds. You may not like some of them but you are forced to deal with them in a professional manner. The work environment can truly train you how to encounter people of all types, while keeping yourself centered in your own positivity.

People come at negativity in many ways and through many guises. Certainly, where I grew up (on the wrong side of the tracks) I saw violence all the time. People would get stabbed or jacked simply because of the color of their skin, the length of their hair, or due to the click somebody thought they were running with. I have seen this type of violence in many other places, via various methods, throughout my life. This style of negativity is above and beyond all that is right. It is pure negativity. We all agree on that. But, it is the subtler forms of negativity that can truly come to affect our lives.

I sometimes think back to this young teenage student I had when I was operating my first martial art studio. Nice kid but he was so dominated by negativity. With every sentence he spoke he knew the sky was going to fall on his head. I had never experienced a person like that before. Though I have met several others since. Though he never set out to intentionally hurt anyone or do anything wrong, simply the energy he embraced and the way he spoke about life to all those he encountered negatively affect everything.

This is a sublet form of negativity, however. It is more psychological and less intentional.

The fact is, as discussed in the previous blog, there is a certain adrenalizing energy that goes hand-in-hand with embracing negativity. People are mad, drunk, pissed off at their boss, unhappy with their life, you name it... But, whatever causes them to embrace negativity, they become empowered by it.

What happens from this is that others who are also angry or disenfranchised are drawn to this type of individual. They cheer on this person as they too are becoming intoxicated with this energy.

Yes, it is invigorating but it only leads to bad things.

Think about a time you encountered someone who was saying something bad about a person. How did that make you feel? Did you become part and parcel of the conversation, becoming intoxicated with the fumes of negativity or did you stop the person and stand up for what is right?

You see, the thing is, people base all of their ideologies about a person upon their own perception of reality. Thus, no one person's opinion about an individual is ever absolutely right or absolutely wrong. Some of these people have become addicted to the drug of negativity, however, so they seek out new ways (i.e. a new person) to focus their negativity upon and get high. And, just like all addictions they continually need more to satisfy their needs. So, they always seek out a new target.

This is the same with people who focus their negativity on the larger scale. The people who hate other religions, other races, or even people who live in a different neighborhood. For someone who seeks out negativity, there will always be something to fuel their craving. But, it must be noted that this is a very bad place to live your life from.

Positivity is so much more sublet then the drug of negativity. Though it certainly has its rewards, particularly in the long run, it is not near as adrenalizing and exhilarating. It is for this reason that people who embrace the path of positivity are commonly much more quiet about their beliefs. And, they rarely stand up to those who scream their negativity to the world. This is not right or wrong, this is simply the way it is. The positive are generally the peaceful.

The issue that should be addressed here and the question that must be asked is, do we let those who are spreading negativity about people and other life things be the only one with a voice? I think not. I think that to, at least, (possibly) countermand their negativity we should call it out. Now, I am not saying physically or verbally confront the person who is spouting negativity. For that is what a negative person thrives on. They want the fight. Especially if it housed somewhere like on the internet where they do not have to actually go hand-to-hand. What I am saying is that they should be called out and put on notice as to what they are doing. They should be told that they are being negative and it is not acceptable and/or appreciated. Yes, they may come back with all of their angered, altered logic which keeps them adrenalizing their internal drug induced state but at least they will be told. From this, other positive people not only can see that they too have a voice but they may chime in, voicing their positive opinion while telling the individual propagating negativity that they are not the only voice that should be heard even though they are most likely the one screaming the loudest.

So, in closing, next time you see negativity being spoken, written, or voiced in life and/or in a magazine, on the internet, or anywhere else, call the person out. Tell them to stop being negative and put a stop to the spreading of negativity.

Moreover, do something positive, write something positive, say something positive. Put positivity out there. It all starts with you.

If you're not the one writing something positive, saying something positive, or doing something positive then who is?

Make the world a better place. Make the world a more positive place.

I Hate That Person
19/04/16 14:11

"I hate that person!"

Have you ever encountered someone who really hated another person? Have you ever hated someone? Have you ever encountered someone who hates someone they have never met? Do you?

"I don't like that person!"

Have you ever encountered someone who really disliked another person? Have you ever disliked someone? Have you ever encountered someone who dislikes someone they have never met? Do you?

"I want to hurt that person!"

Have you ever encountered someone who wants to hurt another person? Have you ever wanted to hurt someone? Have you ever encountered someone who wants to hurt someone they have never met? Do you?

What are the reasons for these emotions?

A person who operates from this perspective may be able to come up with a number of reasons for feeling what they are feeling about another person but how valid are those reasons and from where do they arise? Do they ever take the time to ask themselves, why? Do you?

People decide to place their focus upon someone else when they are not whole and complete onto themselves. They decide to place their focus upon someone else when they are not concentrating upon providing their own contributions to the world.

From thoughts arise emotions. Negative emotions are very adrenalizing. They amp you up. They make you feel invigorated. They make you desire power.

Anger is the king of negative emotions. How much badness has been done to this world based upon anger? Has anything good ever come from anger?

Think about yourself, if these questions find you front and center, how did disliking a person effect your life? What actions did this dislike make you take? What did those actions accomplish? Did they make you a better person? Did your raging emotions make you create something great or do something good? Or, did in make you do something bad?

Here's the catch, some people falsely believe that if they hurt someone they do not like that it is okay. It is not. Hurting only creates further negative emotions and negative actions. From any negative word or negative deed is only born further negativity. And, if it is you who focuses and unleashes that negativity, you will be the one that negativity hunts down.

Did you actually cause harm to the person you didn't like? If you did, what did that accomplish? Did that make you a better person? Ultimately, what did all of those negative emotions equal in your life and the lives of those around you?

When you disliked someone you know or someone you never met, were there others who liked that person? Who was right? Who was wrong?

Think back to a person you didn't like in the past. How much of your time did you spend thinking about that person? How much emotional upheaval did you cause within yourself by thinking about that person? Do you still think about that person? If you don't then there is your proof; your defining factor. Emotions, especially negative emotions, come and go. Though they may emotionally empower you in the moment, as they are based in negativity, they do nothing for the betterment of you or the world. Any actions you take, any words you say, any deeds you accomplish, based upon negativity, only equal a more negative world from where more negative emotions are unleashed.

What do you want to create?

Interaction Based Upon Distraction
19/04/16 12:38

I was in a shop today, kneeling down looking at something on the bottom shelf. A woman, pushing her shopping cart, drives it straight into my ankle. She hit me right in that spot that really hurts when your ankle is impacted. I jump up, *"Ow, Damn it!"* The woman seemed completely oblivious to what she had done. Or, maybe she just didn't care? I looked at her. Finally, she inquires, *"What happened?" "You just hit me in the ankle with your shopping cart!"* But, that was it. She didn't acknowledge what she had done. She didn't say, *"I'm sorry,"* like most of us would have said. She didn't ask if she could help. She just stood there ignoring me and studying what she was considering buying. Now, with my ankle hurting I became very disinterested in buying anything, I state, *"Why don't you open your eyes,"* and I walked away.

Behavior like this, on the part of that woman, is very revealing about life and human interaction. Some people are very caring and conscious about how the impact and interact with the world. Others are not. Certainly, at times, we are each distracted and do something that we didn't mean to do. But, for most of us, those incidences are few and far between. There are other people, however, who perform unconscious actions all the time and simply give it no thought.

People like this may or may not know that they are doing things that impact and/or injure the life of others. Some know and do it anyway. That is simply wrong. Others are so unconscious of their place in life that they do things and are not even aware of them. At best, when confront with this fact, they make excuses or lie. Then, there are those, who like this lady, do something and for whatever reason refuse to take any responsibility for it.

If you live your life in this fashion you are truly living at the lowest level of human consciousness. For any of us to be better and more whole, we must first become a witness to our life and then strive to become the best that we can be. This includes observing and acknowledging all of our action be they good or bad.

Now, one could speculate why a person behaves in this non-remorseful manner. But, at best, that would be guesswork. Each person has their own life motivations and though we can chart and study them it is only that individual person who is ultimately in control of how they behave as they interact with this world.

Most definitely, the majority of us would cast the blame on the person who performs a negative action. But, if they are too locked into their own mind, not caring what they do and/or whom they harm, why would this even matter to them? They don't care what we think and they don't care who they hurt.

One of the great things about long-term training in the martial arts is that it teaches a person to become very aware, even hyperaware, of their environment. As they are constantly schooling their body and their mind to anticipate the next move of their opponent, they become extremely mindful of all that is taking place around themselves. From this, they gain a very profound enhanced perception of the world.

This too is the case with meditation. You can always tell someone who meditates. They are calm, focused, and very aware. They are not lost in an over exaggerated sense of self, thus they are not dominated by anger, greed, lust, desire, and the need to perform hurtful actions whether consciously or not.

Just as you can easy distinguish someone who meditates, you can also recognize someone who does not. People like this are out of control of their emotions, they are ego driven, they think only about themselves, they lie to achieve their desired ends, and they unleash unconscious actions; just like this lady did to me, with no sense of remorse.

Your life is defined by your focus. If you live in a space dominated by desires, denial, and emotions — not caring about whom you harm, then what will be the ultimate outcome of your life? What will happen is that you will pass through life constantly defined by your happiness or your sadness, your anger or your exuberance. You will never know peace as you will not be defined by understanding the greater good. Furthermore, as you are not going out of your way to put your own desires on hold: to elevate the great whole, to do conscious and positive things for other people and this world, then your life will pass by defined only by your selfish, negative, and controversial actions and interactions.

Caring only about yourself is caring only about yourself. That is a very hollow place to base your life upon.

Ask yourself, *"Why are you doing what you are doing?"* Look deep for this answer, don't just pass over it with, *"Because it makes me feel good,"* or something like that. Look deep. Why do you do what you do? Why do you behave the way you behave? How do you interact with other people? Do you care about them? Or, do you only care about yourself and are only interactively nice and responsible when it adds to what you believe is your betterment?

It is very important to step beyond yourself in life. It is very important to stop casting your individualized definitions onto other people. It is very important to care about other people and do good things for them. Most importantly, it is essential to live your life from a place of consciousness; taking others into consideration before you built up a wall around yourself believing that you are the only one that matters, because you are not.

Choose to give before you take. Choose to know yourself and do good things. Choose to never hurt anyone for any reason. Choose to fix what you have broken.

Lose Your Identity, Erase Your History
24/03/16 17:08

The majority of people desire to become SOMETHING. Early in their life they see those who are respected for doing what they do and follow the path of seeking that same admiration. Ask yourself, *"Do you seek to become nothing, to be seen as nothing, to be unknown? Or, do you hope for something more for YOURSELF?"*

People do all that they can to achieve. Though most never find the pathway to find their ultimate dream, they, none-the-less, try to rise to a position of respect and authority within their place of employment, in their community, or at their school.

Most people eventually find the road to marrying and having a family. At that point, the focus of their life quite often shifts from desires for Personal-Self to desires for their child and/or children. *"I want the best for my child. I want them to have a better life than I have had."* How often have you heard those words spoken?

Having a child is not a bad thing. Having desires for one's child is not a bad thing. In fact, having a child often takes the egocentric focus off of the individual allowing them to rise from a life of self-centered thinking to a life of caring and giving. How many of the people you have met, who do not have children, are truly caring and giving people? Most, are simply lost in a Life-Pattern of selfish thought, thinking only about themselves.

Life-Patterns are instigated by the individual. What one does now leads to the next set of available options in one's life. As such, the desire(s) that are pursued defines the entire evolution of a person's life. Though desires may change and what a person does may set a new course of options and availability into motion in a person's life, everything you desire, and everything you do to gain that desire forever defines your life as your life is one continuous emulation of who you want to be leading to what you are.

Think about the actions you have taken to achieve your desires and your dreams. Have they hurt anyone? Have they hurt you? Are you proud of them? Do they make you ashamed? Do they make you happy or do they make you sad? Remember, you wanted something, you went about achieving that something, thus, it was you who set your ALL into motion by wanting what you wanted, desiring what you desired, which means you are personally responsible for all the goodness and/or all the damage you created in that pursuit. If you hurt anyone in that pursuit you will be forever bound to that person as you did what you did and their life evolution was changed because of it. Remember that.

The thing about personal achievement is that most of the achieved have not cared about their personal effect. They only think about themselves and achieving their desire and thus, the thought of damage to others rarely, if ever, comes to mind. As much as the person of consciousness will say, *"This selfish mindset is not the attitude one should possess,"* this has been one of the key traits of humanity since its evolution to the realms of thoughtful-self. People only think about themselves and what they want!

Now that this has been established, let's turn this scenario around a little bit. What if you desired nothing? What if you wanted to be nothing? What if you did not care about your position or your legacy? How would you be feeling right now? What would you have done differently in your life? What would you not be regretting? Who would you have not hurt? Who would you have not been hurt by?

If you did not want to be something, if you did not do the things you have done to be that SOME-THING how would your life have evolved differently?

The fact is, in life we can never go back in time. We never get a re-do. But, what we can do is to become conscious enough to look deeply into the patterns of life and learn from not only our evolutionary movement but the evolutionary movements of all those around us. We can open our eye.

If you can take a moment and step away from yourself and your desire(s) long enough to truly witness what is going on with your life, the lives of those you interact with, and the lives of the Greater-All, then you have the chance to become more than your limited, selfish self. Instead of possessing a desire for your life to be some idealized ego-driven machine, adored by the masses, you have the chance to truly do something good for the world by becoming something that no one else can see or worship, a True Being not driven by ego and desire.

Most people don't want this. Most people don't understand this. Most people if they heard about it simply dismiss it as nonsense. They do this because they are so locked into the realms of their own identity, of their desire to become what they desire, that they are too lost to understand that they will never achieve what their mind sees. Why? Because what is, *"Out There,"* is never *"In Here,"* it is all an illusion. What you see other people BE-ING is never what you can BE because you are not them, just as they are not you. What you see out there is a projection of an idealized reality you have fantasied in your mind. It is not real. At best, it is only what you hope it will be.

By comprehending this you allow yourself to realize that all that you hope to be, all the steps you take to get there, are, at best, simply your projected desires where you attempt to live a reality that may never be had. Thus, your desires to BE are nothing more than a Self-Instigated Illusion.

Knowing this, you have one of two choices to make. …Two choices that now you can make very consciously. One, are you going to continue on the path you are on, doing what you are doing, damaging who what you are damaging? Two, are you going to let go and simply BE? By being, you become free. Your desires are let go so you create nothing:

no bad, no good. From here, you can be happy and whole within yourself. From here, no one is hurt, thus, you are not re-hurt. You are complete free and not trapped by the hurt that arises from not having what you want.

Freedom is always a better perfection that a life bound by desire. You are you. YOU is all YOU will ever be.

Do you want to be happy in your freedom? Or, do you want to be tormented by what you desire?

The Holder of Your Secrets
24/03/16 17:07

In each of our lives we do what we do. Some of these, *"Done Things,"* we are very proud of and want the world to know about them; others — not so much. Some things we do are private; we want to keep them a secret.

Many of these, *"Secrets,"* are sealed. As no one saw or heard them so they are locked only into our mind and/or the mind of the person we performed them with. This is life…

There is the other side of the issue, however. Sometimes are secrets are found out. …Someone else saw them, heard them, or researched them. From this, at the discretion of <u>another,</u> they can be released to the world.

There have been tape recorders and cameras forever. Video tape cameras have been around for a long while. Now, everyone carries all three of them on their phone. From this, personal secrets have become very hard to keep.

Most people do not set out to capture your secrets. Unless you are doing something bad to someone or something, your secrets are never sought out, as no one cares. In other cases, it is happenstance. You do something bad (something you want to keep a secret from the world) and what you say or do is so loud your secret is accidentally captured. Then what?

The fact is, people only keep secrets because they wish to hide who they truly are from other people. …They wish to hide what they truly do from others. Why? Because, in most cases, they wish to be seen a certain way by certain people. They wish to be seen as something they are not. They wish to be perceived in a specific light by a specific group of people. Whether this group is large or small is unimportant, it is simply defined by the mind of the individual who wishes others to not know who they truly are and what they truly do.

But, why is this? This mindset exists because people are not truthful about themselves — they are not truthful to themselves; for if they were there would be no need for secrets. If a person would not be attempting to project a persona, if they would simply be who and what they are, then there would be no need to hide anything.

Some people want to reveal and spread the secrets of another person. Some people make this their life quest. Some people lie about other people, pretending that they are telling someone's secrets when all they are doing is telling a lie.

The fact is, finding out someone's secrets is invigorating. ...You know what you're not suppose to know. You know what someone didn't want you know. From this, you feel empowered. You feel you have power over that person. Think about how many negative life events have been set into motion by those who possess this mindset?

In this modern world, your secret(s) may now be easily captured. But, what if you have no secretes? Then, who would care?

Secrets are you hiding the truth about you from someone/anyone. If you existing in a space of being one-hundred percent yourself — one hundred percent honest about yourself, then what secrets would your life hold? You would be free.

Stop lying about who you truly are. Stop hiding who you truly are. Stop doing bad things. Then, you are free as you have no secrets. From this, not only does your world become freer are but the entire world becomes just a little bit better.

How is that Buddhism?
14/09/15 16:58

I am never one to criticize a person's religion. I believe, we all believe what we believe, created by an untold number of influences, and that is the way it has always been. Occasionally, however, an individual brings their beliefs to the forefront of our conversation and it forces me to think…

Recently, I was speaking with a young girl I know and she told me that she was, *"Getting into Buddhism."* She went on to tell me that one of her family members had continue to suggest that she do so and finally she took the plunge. *"Great,"* I exclaimed.

Then, she began to tell me about how one of the teachers of her group had told her to define three things that she really wanted and begin to focus on them as she chanted. *"Nichiren Shōshū,"* I knowingly questioned. *"Yes. How did you know that,"* she asked. Well, she may not have known, but I am sure all of you know, that I have been walking this path for a long-long time, so my studies and my interactions are pretty vast in the spiritual realms and since my early time on the path forward, *Nichiren Shōshū* has been around.

Now, I am not going to discuss *Nichiren Shōshū* in this piece, for their formation, who, and what they are, is documented out there far better that I could ever abbreviate. And, at the core of their teachings is a very profound scripture, T*he Lotus Sutra*. What I will say, however, is that ever since I first encountered this group some forty years ago, their main focus for bringing people into their fold is to promise the obtainment of a person's desire by chanting this group's primary mantra, *"Namu Myōhō Renge Kyō."* This too was the case with my young friend.

One of the most profound and simple teachings that the Buddha taught was, *"The cause of suffering is desire."* For me, this is the essence of Buddhism. If we look to the root of any problem we encounter we will easily see that is/was based upon a desire that we had; either for something, someone, to feel a certain way, or to experience life in a specific manner. The questions then arises, *"How does any branch of Buddhism teach a path to the obtainment of desire when one of its foundational understanding is that, the cause of suffering is desire?"*

Now, I am not saying that their technique does not work. I think we all can agree, the focusing on something and the consciously taking steps to obtaining it is the best way to actualize any desire. But, how is that Buddhism? Buddhism is about the developed lack of desire, not the obtainment of it.

In any case, as always, I let it go. I said nothing and let her walk down her own path, eventually finding her own realizations.

There were a couple of things that were additionally interesting about our conversation, however. She told me that she almost instantly obtained one of her desires. She wanted to play guitar and sing in public and one of her friends had invited her to a coffee house where that type of event took place. Once there, she got up and played.

It made me realize, if all of our desires were that easily obtainable, how easy our life would be. And, this is the thing to keep in mind as we walk down the road to obtaining our desires. If our desires are easily obtainable then, though we may not be free from desire, at least we will not be damned by wishing for things that we will never obtain.

Others
14/09/15 16:58

I imagine that we each have had people come into our lives and really mess things up for us. Had we invited them in, then it would have been our own fault and there would be no one to blame but ourselves. But, this is not commonly the case for once we know of a person's prediction for negativity, lying, deceiving, cheating, uncontrolled behavior, and doing other bad things; we very consciously shun them. But then, there is the other life-scenario — there is the case when someone intrudes his or her way into our life, forces their way in, and then by their deeds and actions all we are left with is the life damage and life destruction that they have created.

Hopefully, these experiences will be few and far between in one's life. But, the fact of the matter is, no matter how few or how far better these life interactions are, once they have occurred, all we are left with is the never ending memory of the damage another person has caused us.

Most people do not set out to hurt others. Though some are of this mindset and intentionally devise a scheme to harm others, they are the worst of the worst; all of their acts are criminal and eventually they pay the price for them. But, more often then not, the people that damage our lives are those who are too unconscious, too self-centered, too unaware, too full of themselves, too much in self-denial and self-deceit and possessing too much unjustified self-importance to even fully comprehend or care about what they are doing. Once they have done what they have done, they lie, they deny, they live in a state of self-imposed superiority so that they will not have to accept that they are truly a bad person, doing wrong things to the lives of others.

In fact, have you ever encountered the situation where a person did a really bad thing to your life and then they tried to turn it around on you and blame you for your reactions based upon their negative actions? This is one of the prime examples of a person who is completely out of touch with the reality of what they are doing to the life of another person. But, people like this are everywhere; lost in their own self-deception and hoping to damage further the life of a person that they already damaged.

Truthfully, it is very sad… Sad, because the lives of the people they negatively affected are affected forever. The person's life experience, their life chances, and their next level of life opportunities are damaged forever. But, what does the person who instigated the damage do to correct anything that they have done? Commonly, the answer to that is nothing. They lie and they deny. They run away from the truth about who and what they are. And, as previously stated, in some cases, they even attempt to blame the victim for their own actions of instigation. These people are simply bad and nothing that they can say or do will ever change this fact. They cannot change this fact unless they choose to go to source of their problem and undo all the negativity they have unleashed. But commonly, they are too egomaniacal to even attempt this feat.

And, here lies the ultimate definition of a person's life; does that individual try to fix what they have broken?

In life, most people are good. They try to do good things and attempt to exist in space of harming no one. They are not locked into a mindset of self-deception where they tell themselves that are something that they are not. If they do unintentionally damage the life of another person, they turn their ego off and they do whatever it takes to repair that damage, for they know that damage will haunt their evolution forever if they do not correct it.

The good are truthful to themselves and others. The bad live in a space of denial and self-deception, not caring about others.

In life, though we all want what we want, we all want to do what we want to do, it is essential that we think about our environment and others first before we do anything. For is we do not, our words, our deeds, and our actions can hurt others because we did not take <u>others</u> into consideration before we performed said actions.

Others are the fact of life. There are others all around us, all of the time. We must think of others first, before we think of ourselves if we hope to live a good life.

In some cases, some people are too self-absorbed to hear or comprehend these words. They believe that it is okay to do whatever it is they are doing, as it is their means to their ends. It may get them money, notoriety, physiological release, or psychological empowerment. But, the root and the heart of the problem, in thinking about life in that fashion, is that it is all based upon the concept of ME. And ME, is a very selfish place to live at.

Others are the key to life as it will be others who define your life.

What have you done to others? Did you hurt others? No matter what your justification for doing what you did may have been, did you undo any hurtful action, did you fix the damage you created, or did you simply live in a web of self-deceit? The answer to that question will define your entire existence.

Others define your life. How did you treat others?

They're the Ones Talking About Me
I'm Not the One Talking About Them
14/09/15 16:58

Long ago I coined the statement, *"You know you're famous when people you've never met say things about you that aren't true."* This came about when I read an article someone had written about me that was full of unsubstantiated falsehoods and flat out untruths. Yet, the person who wrote it had the appearance of being credentialed in his field and presented the paper in a very formulated format. Though the reading of it amused me to no end, I later begin to contemplate how someone who didn't know me and read it would believe the false words to be fact, not fiction. And, here is where the problem(s) begin...

Ever since I first began writing poetry, novels, articles, books, painting, and making music and movies, people began to draw conclusions about me. This is a fact of life, when you create, people who love, hate, or don't care about what you create are going to come to their own conclusions about your work and yourself; be they true or false.

In times gone past, opinions were kept to one's circle of friends. If you were going to send your opinion about a person or their creation to a magazine, more times than not, the magazine would fact-check the writing before it was ever published. This is the world I grew up in. Throughout my studies at the various universities I attended and later when I began to be published as a journalist and an author, what I wrote had to possess a verifiable factual essence. You had to prove what you said. Then came the age of the Internet and the publish-on-demand world of printing. Anybody could say anything and there is no one there to challenge what a person says. Sure, you can get into twitter wars with a person but what is the point? People believe what they choose to believe, whether it be true or not.

The fact is, in today's world, when someone says something about somebody that is not based in fact, the lie simply continues to spread. I have seen one person say something about me that was completely untrue and then I have seen that same statement quoted by another and another. All false, yet it is presented as if it were the truth, when it is not.

This is the thing about the life of the creative… The creative, create. The others talk about those who create.

Whenever I teach a class or a seminar I always pose the question to my students, *"Who do you want to be? The creative or those who talk about the creative?"*

In a world where you can say anything about anybody with little consequence, the only person you are beholden to is yourself and the karmic destiny you lay out that will unfold in front of you based upon your deeds, actions, and words. Therefore, it is you who must ask the question of yourself, *"Are you a person who speaks of others, expounding your opinions about an individual based upon your own appraisal of their words and creations or are you a person who is the source of your own creations?"* Yes, being the source point of your own creations will put you in the bull's-eye but it will be something wholly you own. If, on the other hand, you spent your time focused upon analyzing the creations of others and the personage of who created them, all you are doing is further spreading the myth of that individual.

If you speak the truth that is the truth, then the truth will be known and the truth will embrace you. If you spread the lie, based upon your judgment(s), then all you will be known as is a liar once the truth is revealed and all you will be defined as is an individual who relished in the limelight of others.

You Are A Liar
14/09/15 16:57

Not only am I often asked to speak and write about the subject of truth, I am quite frequently confounded with the realities of life when someone lies to me. To begin this discussion I must state that ever since I was a very young boy I had this uncanny ability to know when someone was lying to me. In my early years I used to confront people with this fact, *"You are a liar,"* or, *"You are lying."* I quickly came to understand that this was not the best method to keep any conversation or relationship moving forward. So, since then, I pretty much just let people keep talking — even if I know that they are lying to me.

At the central core of all that is right and good with life is the truth. But, what is the truth? The truth is not something big, grand, or abstract, the truth is the essence of who we each are. Where does truth come from? It comes from us. We are each the source or the truth or the lies. From truth, goodness is given birth to. From lies, all badness emulates.

People lie for all kinds of reasons. They lie to be seen as something more than they actually are. They lie to get something that they desire. They lie to protect themselves. And, the list goes on... But, at the central core of who and what a person truly is, the question must be raised, *"Are they a liar?"* Are you? Do you lie? It does not matter the reason or your reasoning? Are you a liar? If you are, all that you will ever be is a liar. For all things that you do and say set the next evolution of life into motion; not only for your life but also for all of those whom interact with you. If anything that you say or do is instigate from a lie, then there can never be truth. For without a basis in truth there can never be a greater good. A lie never equals the truth.

Most people, when they are confronted with the fact that they have lied will either re-lie, attempting to cover up their initial lie, or they will make all kinds of excuses for why they lied — providing all kinds of justifications for their action. But, again, this is not the truth. This is only exaggerating any lie that they already told.

If a person lies to you, they can never be trusted because they were willing to lie to you in the first place. If a person is willing to lie to you, (and justify their actions either to themselves or to you), they are not an honest person. A dishonest person is a liar, no matter what justification they are providing themselves with for doing what they are doing and saying what they are saying.

Life is a very simple place. The truth is the sole defining factor of all interpersonal relationships and with a person's individual ability to achieve higher consciousness. Think about this, if a person lies to others, if a person lies to himself or herself, do you think they have the ability to obtain higher consciousness? No, they do not. A lie is never the truth, no matter what. If you lie you have tied yourself to the lower level of desire-filled human consciousness and you will never obtain what you hope to achieve for you have poisoned your own well.

As is always the case, the world begins with you. All you say and do affects the all and the everything of the further evolution of this place we call life. If you are lying, for any reason, that means that you are personally responsible for damaging the greater good.

I understand that most people don't want to hear this and that many people do not even care. But, if you care about humanity, if you care about the greater good, if you care about your own self and your ultimate life-legacy, do not lie. For all lying does is create a world based upon falsehoods and deception. Stop making excuses to yourself for lying and become more. By you become more, via the truth, the entire world becomes better.

The truth is the ultimate defining factor for life. If you lie, stop it. If you have lied, undo your lies. Mostly, stop lying to yourself that your lying is justified. Stop being a liar!

When You've Done Nothing Wrong or Have You?
24/09/15 16:56

Life is a curious conglomerate of actions and interactions. People are all around us. From this, we are set to encounter them in various ways throughout our lifetime. Some of these encounters are pleasant but some are not. In the instances that are less than ideal, we are thrown into the pit of disarray and though we had no desire to encounter this type of life interaction we are forced to do just that.

Negative life interactions can come at us in any number of ways. The one defining factor is that it is certain that we would have never wanted the occurrence to occur in the first place.

The list of these undesired interactions are as long as life itself. And, as we travel though life's passageway, we will each encounter them to varying degrees. Though we may try to protect ourselves from them, there is no way to emerge unscathed — having never encountered one.

In some cases, these interactions are accidents on the part of the person unleashing them. For example, most people who get into auto accidents do not desire to do so. But then, there are the people who are simply unconscious participants of life and they do not think about others. Instead, they only think about themselves. These people are perhaps the most dangerous in that they are not even aware of what they are unleashing upon another person. When confronted with this fact, for the most part, all an individual who behaves in this manner will do is deny any responsibly and/or make excuses for their actions. At the root of their essence, an individual who operates from this mindset, is simply wrong — they live life focused only upon themselves and do not care what they do to others or what events they set into motion.

Finally, there is the person who performs wrong acts, on others, very consciously and by design. These people are the criminals, the egomaniacs, the sociopaths, and the insane. Though we each, no doubt, attempt to avoid people of this caliber, at times in our life we may be forced to come into contact with them and from this, and based upon their actions, our life may never the same.

At the heart of life interaction(s) and the consequence(s) based upon those interactions, we who walk the path of consciousness must come to terms with how to encounter all life events and move forward once one of these undesired life occurrences has taken place. From this, though we may not be the one responsible for setting a life event into motion, we may emerge stronger and wiser from having encountered it.

For each event, the reaction to the action will be somewhat different and there is no one universal method for how to deal with all of them. The primary thing that should be accomplished, however, is that you walk away having been the most that you can be and having encountered the person or persons and informed them they did something wrong. Post that, the best you can hope for is that life can move on.

Now, here arises a problem, many people live their life in a constant state of denial and justification. Though they may be very wrong and have set a negative course of events into motion, many will deny it to their dying day — especially to the face of those whom they have injured or to the ears of anyone whom will listen to them. This does not take away or diminish what they have done; however, it is simply a constant of the existence for those people who base their life upon living in a state of denial.

The fact of human existence is, many people are willing to lie, at any moment, in order to protect themselves from what they believe will occur if they own up to the truth. This is not right but it is the way life is.

Liars are unconscious contributors to this life-space but they are everywhere. This being understood, you cannot define your reaction and ultimate recuperation by framing your existence upon the truth or the lies that come out of the mouth of the person who has caused you to encounter a negative life experience. Instead, you must express your dissatisfaction; via whatever method you may have, and then move forward to the best of your ability in your life.

But, life is complicated. Everyone has a reason for his or her reason. It is at this point that life becomes convoluted.

Let's look at a few examples to hopefully gain a deeper understanding of the cause and the causation factor for the unleashing of negative life events, what can occur from them and how you could behave if you experience one.

Recently, here in the States, a group of African-American women were taking a wine tasting train ride through the California wine country, enjoying their wine, and having a grand old time. A grand old time, so much so, that they became very loud in their laughter and joylessness. As they were on a train with numerous other people who began to complain about their loudness, they were initially nicely asked to tone down their voices and their exuberance. Perhaps due to the alcohol, they did not. Thus, the train stopped and police officers escorted them off. From this, rose the call of racism.

The news channels all ran stories on this occurrence. The talking heads spoke, some claimed, *"Racism!"* Others stated, *"African-Americans are louder and should be left alone because that is simply the way they are."* Some said, *"If they were white, this would not have happened."* But, that is not true. Have you ever been around someone who is very loud and they are destroying the atmosphere you paid for? Black or White, you do not care. The fact is, we each need to be conscious of our actions and behave in an appropriate manner in accordance with where we find ourselves. This is life. If you are not, you set negative life occurrences into motion and negatively affect the lives of those around you. Thus, it is you who is to blame, not the person who complained about your unacceptable actions.

For example, I know this oftentimes overly exuberant, young white male. He and his friends got onto an airplane. When the stewardess was demonstrating how to put on the life vest, he got up and began to mimic her. Yes, it was in fun but it was not appropriate for the environment where he and his friends found themselves. As such, they were evicted from the plane and ban from ever flying on that airline again. Racism? No, simply an appropriate reaction to an action?

Here lies the issue; most of us are conscious and try to be appropriate in all of our life actions and interactions. We think before we act. Other, however, are either uncaring or unconscious. From this, they perform inappropriate actions that negatively affect the lives of others.

In life, we must each be conscious of what we do and whom we do it to. We must study our environment and think before we act. This is the definition of a conscious individual.

There is also the other side of the issue, the place where people attempt to overreach with any power they may have in order to establish their placement in society and the food chain. To illustrate, I will tell you of a small life encounter that I had a few months ago that was both amusing and angering for I was accosted but I had done nothing wrong.

I was leaving a store that I had shopped in for years-upon-years. I was carrying the few items I had purchased out to my car. Just as I was about to open my truck, I hear a voice behind me, *"Hello, hello!"* I turn and it was the store manager. I questioned, *"Me?"* Yes, he wanted me.

To cut to the chase, a new employee had seen me walking out of the store with my items. As I try to do all I can for the environment, in any small way I can, I generally say, *"No,"* to plastic bags and simple carry my purchased items out in my hands. The new employee, not knowing me, assumed I had stolen them. I mean it wasn't like I was looking all sketchy or anything. There I was, fifty-six years old, wearing a Hugo Boss sport coat, three-hundred dollar Nike tennis shoes, a Rolex, I had a pocket full of money, and I am being accused of stealing — this, by a man, (the manager), who knows me very well. He asked me to come back into the store and show him my receipt in the presence of the other employee. Which I did. I then walked back to my car and put my items in my truck.

By my nature, I am always amused at life. I forever see the ridiculousness of action, reaction, and human nature. So, my initial emotion was amusement. But, then that emotion began to change. I became angry. Who were these people to accuse me of stealing? Me, someone who has never stolen anything in my entire life! I walked back in and confronted the manager. He apologized but what does an apology really mean and what does it truly repair. It is simply words. And words have no true meaning. Action is the only true test in life.

Having done all I could do, based upon anger and condemnation, I left the store. What else could I do? I decided to never return. And, that is sad for I truly enjoyed going to that shop.

You see, here lies the essence of this discourse; even though the truth is, you have done nothing wrong, people set life events into motion all around you, all for the time, and you are the one who is forced to deal with them. Whether it is the loud person who is thrown off of the train or a person who accuses you of a crime that you did not committee, the people who set negative actions into motion are the ones who are responsible, yet, you are the one left dealing with the consequences. In some instances, these are minor events and the emotions and the life reactions that they cause are quickly forgotten. In other cases, they may come to define your entire future. Though you were not the one at fault, you did nothing wrong, you are none-the-less the person whose life has been changed due to the actions of another.

One of the African-America women, who had the aforementioned experience on the wine-train, claimed she would never be the same. And, I get it. If you were pulled off a train that you were having loads-and-loads of fun on by police officers, that would be pretty traumatizing. But, who's fault was it? Had her group kept their interactions to an appropriate level, they would have had no problems with the other passengers and they would not have been escorted off of the train.

Get loud, you call attention to yourself. When you're loud, if the people around you don't want to hear what you have to say, there will be consequences.

Life is complicated. Like I have long, semi-jokingly stated, *"Enlightenment is easy. It's life that's hard."*

So, as we pass though life and we encounter these events, it is essential to make the right decisions in the moments they occur. Because here is the fact, the person who has done something negative to you or set a negative course of events into motion is probably either not going to care, feel that they had the justification to do so, or play the victim card and claim that their face, their race, their thoughts, or their mind were infringed upon. Or, they will simply lie. Thus, what are you left with? You will never be able to gain true redemption without having that life event; they set in motion, undone. But, it never can be undone. At best, all you will have is your appropriate reaction to their action. Then, you will need to move along not holding on to what another person has done to your life as best as you can. From this, no matter where or by whom a life event was instigated, during your existence, you will be able to maintain control and put your own definition upon it.

That's the best you can hope for.

What You Said. What You Should've Said. What You Didn't Say.
24/09/15 16:21

Life interactions are based upon communication. We communicate to say what we want, get what we want, express our feelings on a particular subject, and to state our happiness or dissatisfaction with a life-situation or life-event.

Communication is one of the most natural forms of the human experience. We learn to communicate at a very early age. How we communicate, how we express our thoughts and our feelings is initially programmed into us by the way those around us communicate. Generally, we first learn how to express our thoughts, feelings, and desires by the way our parents and our other family members communicate. This is why those individuals who rise out of a loud, boisterous family generally communicate in loud patterns. On the other hand, those who come from a quiet, contemplative family-scape generally are must subtler in their forms of expression and communication.

Once we have had the basic foundations of our communication skills taught to us by our parents and siblings we then move forward and develop our own unique methods of communication guided by our individual personalities. It is quite common to understand that an adult that uses yelling and screaming to express what they are feeling found that as a child they could get want they wanted if they cried and threw a tantrum. On the other hand, if an individual allows people to rant and rave but does not become involved in their confrontational communications it can then easily be understood that they subconsciously learned, early in life, that expressing one's self in this manner does not lead to any desired end. Thus, they remain passive with their communication skills.

In life, we each are provided with the ability to speak our thoughts. This is, of course, tempered by where we find ourselves in history and to which socioeconomic, political, or religious backdrop we are born.

Once we understand the definition of our communication skills, and which way of communicating is most beneficial and rewarding to our life, we then move forward and say what we say guided by our beliefs, our ego, and our understanding of interpersonal relationships. Some people are very conscious and thoughtful in how they communicate, other are rude, unthinking, and judgmental in all that they say. Who are you? And, are you honest with yourself in the way you communicate and how your communications are interpreted by other people? The fact is, many people are so lost in their exaggerated sense of Self that they do not even take the time to consider how the manner in which they communicate is affecting others that they speak with and/or the world around them as a whole.

In each of our lives we express how we feel — we say what we say. How many times have you said something that you wish you had not said? How many times have you said something that you believed came out wrong? How many times have you, once you have expressed something that you believed came out wrong or was not a correct or righteous expression of your thoughts, did you work to correct what you said? The answer to these questions provides you with deep insight into how you view the world, how you view yourself, and whether or not you have a truly respectful understanding of life and the lives of those that exist around. For, if more times than not you stand firm in what you have said, even if it was hurtful to someone/anyone or anything then this fact alone allows you to peer into yourself and see that you are a very self-centered individual. Moreover, if you do not care how what you have said affects other people and life events, it tells you that you exist in a space of vanity and unaware self-righteousness; sociopathy if you will. From this insight and understanding it allows you, if nothing else, to understand how you perceive this world. It also tells you that you may need to take a look at yourself, how you perceive others, and how you will be remembered because your life is defined through your words and your actions.

Aside from simply what we say, when we communicate, and how we say it, there are times in the midst of conversations when we realize the direction in which the conversation is heading and we consciously choose to not say what we internally wish to say. This is called, *"Discretion,"* and it is one of the highest forms of selfless, interactive human understanding. …You know what you want to say. …You know what you could say is the truth. …But, you choose not to say it because the truth, at least in that particular situation, will only cause the discussion you are involved with to progress towards the realms of negativity.

The thing about human existence is, many people are so lost within their own lying-mind that they do not have the ability to truly look within themselves and to see or care about what effect they are having on others. From this is born the mindset of irrational justification for a person's thoughts, words, and actions. Therefore, to not fall prey to this selfish mindset you can simply employee your own internal sense of discretion. From this conscious action you are left <u>whole</u> and self-aware enough to not have to express what you think in order to make yourself be seen as something more and/or better. This is a true state of self-actualization.

Many interpersonal conversations are based upon one person trying to make their thoughts and their feelings more prominent and more definitive than the other person or persons. But, this is not true interactive conversation. This is ego. And, many people base their entire form of conversation upon attempting to project that they know more, that they are more right than the other person(s) involved in the conversation. I am sure we have all interacted with people like this. But, if we possess enough interpersonal wisdom to not have to prove that our point is the right point then this is where a true understanding of interactive human consciousness comes into play.

This fact is much harder to emulate when you are in a conversation with a person who has or is doing bad things. When they are hurting you and/or other people via their conscious or unconscious actions. Then, the term, *"Bite your tongue,"* really comes into play because though you posses the discretion to not need to win every discussion you enter into, what they are doing is simply wrong, and though you may want to express the truth via your words, your higher-self keeps you from doing so.

As is the case with all life, we each rethink what we have done or said once an unsavory situation has occurred. This too is the case with interpersonal conversations, especially when you have been forced to interact with an individual exhibiting lower consciousness by lying, changing the facts, or misrepresenting the truth. "I should have said…," is a common thought when we internalize these conversations after the fact. None-the-less, it is up to you to be more than that person, not fret about what you didn't say, and move on and away from this type of individual as a person like this is their own worst enemy and is setting up the pathway for their own lack of life-fulfillment and self-destruction by not only being dishonest in their words but thereby projecting their own sense of lack of self-awareness to the entire world.

Conversation is at the root of human grown and expanding understandings. It also provides you with a microscope to view into the mind of those you are conversing with.

Know yourself. Know your own mind. Refine your interactive skillset and move forward into the world never spreading falsehood, only speaking your own truth in the most palatable manner possible.

Word lead to actions. What actions do you want to instigate?

Are You Controlling Your Anger or is Your Anger Controlling You?
24/09/15 16:18

In our lives it is inevitable that each of us will encounter situations that we are not happy with. These situations can be defined by all kinds of variables but at the root of all of them is the fact that their occurrence makes us unhappy.

The question must be asked, *"Where does our unhappiness arise from?"* The answer to that question is quite simple — where dissatisfaction arises from is our desire for a particular life-situation to be played out in a certain manner of our choosing, but it is not.

Many people, when encountering a life situation that makes them unhappy, observe it for what it is. Yes, they may be become unhappy, frustrated, depressed, or even angry but they do not express these emotions in an unsavory manner. They may tell the person who is causing the situation that they are unhappy or even angry with what they are doing but they are mature enough to know that most life situations are not so important to allow the emotions that they evoke to move forward from that moment and define an entire life. Meaning, any actions you take when you are dissatisfied or angry should not be so all-encompassing that they may come to defining the rest of your existence or negatively influence the existence of any other person.

The truth be told, the majority of this world's population is very selfish. People are out for themselves — they only think about themselves or those they care about and the rest of the world be damned. For those of us who walk the path of consciousness we may believe that this is the wrong way to encounter the world. None-the-less, this is the way it is. And, though we may hope to raise the overall consciousness of the world by us being the best person we can be, the majority of humanity does not possess this mindset. So, what are we left with? We are left with a world defined by individual desire and people acting out whenever their personal desires are not being met.

How do you act when you are not happy? How do you act when you are not getting what you want? How do you behave when you are angry? The answer to these questions is not only what sets the course for your own existence into motion but it also, at least partially, defines the lives of all those people whom interact with you. And, from there, it moves outwards to all of those people who interact with those people you have interacted with.

Here is a fact, few people ever take into consideration how what they are doing and how they are behaving is affecting their own evolution let-alone the lives of others whenever they are acting-out in an unenlightened manner.

How you behave in any given moment, how you react to your desires either being met or not being met, projects from you out onto the entire world. If, when are angry, you study this emotion and come to a deeper understanding of SELF, the world becomes a better place. This is because of the fact that you, personally, have become a more aware individual. If, on the other hand, you explode with your uncontrolled anger whenever you are not happy with the cards life has dealt you, this means that not only have you affected your own inner evolution in a negative manner but you have also negatively affect the lives of all those around you by not controlling your angry outbursts and irrational behavior. From this, not only have you personally become defined by your explosive nature but you make the lives of all of those people around you, whom you have forced to become aware of and interactive with your anger, much worse.

If you want to keep YOU as the central focus of all your thoughts and actions understand this, if you have hurt anyone by your actions or your behavior, no matter whether consciously or unconsciously, you have hurt yourself. That is what karma is.

Ultimately, you are the source point of the rest of the world! If you understand this, then you become much more thoughtful about allowing your emotion to be in control of you as opposed to you being in control of them.

Again, it must be stated, most people don't care. They do what they do with complete disregard for others. They feel they are justified in their emotions, deeds, and actions. If confronted with the fact of what they have done or how they have behaved is negatively affect the lives of others, at best, they will simply make excuses for their actions and/or claim they have the right to feel the way they want to feel — to behave the way they want to behave. They may even attempt to turn the scenario around on the individual who is expressing to them how their negative emotional actions are hurtful to the lives of others. But, all this is based upon are the excuses of an unenlightened individual who has allowed their emotions to run ramped and come to control them.

This is the source point for the dilemma of human emotion. People are emotional creatures. People find justification for their actions. People try to blame others, god, and life, for the way they are feeling. If a person has become entrenched in negative emotional behavior and/or negative emotional outbursts, they find some-one or some-philosophy to give them a logical and justifiable justification for the way they are behaving. What they do not do, however, is looking deeply within themselves, see that they are living their life in a negative manner, and thereby come to fix their internal psychological apparatus.

So, what can you, (as the person who chooses to live a life of positive consciousness), do? First of all, if you are one of those people who is defined by frustration and anger, take a long hard look at your life. Find out what you are dissatisfied or angry about. Most probably you will come to the conclusion that it is based upon you not getting the things you want, being with the people you want, achieving the goals you have set for yourself, or living the life and the lifestyle you had envisioned for yourself. Okay, so now you know. Now what? Here is the thing, you can work towards your dreams, but if working towards your dreams is based upon a mindset of anger, your dreams will be defined by anger-filled accomplished if they are ever lived at all. If you based your life upon constantly embracing the negative emotions of frustration and anger, all you will encounter is defeat — which will probably lead you to more anger. Why? Because not only have you locked yourself into constantly embracing a negative and self-defeating emotion but due to this emotion you have negatively affect the lives of all those you have encounter. Yes, you can lie to them and pretend to be something you are not. But, at the root of all personal growth and self-actualization is to embrace who you truly are, refine that inner being as necessary, and then project that positivity to the world. If you are good, you will be seen as good. If you have helped people and not hurt people, those who can help you will be more willing to do so. But, if you hurt yourself and hurt other through your unrelenting anger and frustration, what image and what energy do you think you are projecting to the world?

 Negative only equals negativity. If you focus your life based upon negative emotions, you project those emotions from your inner being onto all those you interact with. No lie will hide the truth and only negativity can be born from negativity.

 Life begins and ends with you. This is YOUR life. How are you going to live it? Is it going to be defined by your anger and your frustrations — letting those negative emotions emulate from you and define all of your personal life-space and relationships? Or, are you going to become MORE, are you going to delve into the essence of your being, analyzing and overcoming all negativity, fix any negativity you have unleashed, and not let something so temporary as an emotion come to define the definition of you to the world?

Was Your Life Better a Year Ago?
24/09/15 16:14

"Was your life better a year ago?"
This is a question that I believe each person should ask himself or herself.

I think that we all know people; we have all met people who the first things they talk about is what they are going through and how things are bad or a least not as good as they were back then. What they are doing is comparing their life now to how their life was then. And, that's fine. Verbalizing what you feel to friends and family is all-good as long as it doesn't bring everybody down. Maybe this is you. But, though many people feel what they feel about what is going on in their life, few people ever take the time to study the reason why. Few people have the ability to truly look in the mirror and give themselves a true appraisal of what is going on in their life and why. They may justify their actions, they may blame others, they may attribute their current, less than perfect circumstances, to any number of reasons but what they rarely do is blame themselves.

All of your life is based upon what you have done. If you hurt others, you are a fault. If you damage things, you are at fault. If you lie, cheat, deceive, steal, you are at fault. Even if you believe you have a right to do the things you have done, if your life was better a year ago from where it is today, you must have done something wrong.

This is not about karma, self-guilt, or anything like that. For, the fact of the matter is, most people feel no guilt for what they have done — they could care less if they hurt or damage people or things. They feel they are entitled to do what they do when they do it and that is that. Again, few people possess the ability to take a long hard look at themselves in the mirror.

If your life is not on the path you desire; if your life is not fulfilled and abundant, if you are not living the way you want, then who else is to blame but you? You did what you did. You set a course of events into motion. Thus, you have ended up where you have ended up solely based upon what you have done.

Some people are not as selfish, unconscious, or as self-serving as the greater whole. Some people actually care enough to care. But, these people also, at times, find themselves living a life that is not ideal. But, why is this? Why is this if a person tries to give back? Commonly this occurs, in a giving person, due to the fact that they are giving from a space of ego. *"I am this." "I am giving to you." "It is I who has this to give to you." "I am doing this for you."* The central precept here is, *"I." "I"* is about ego. *"I"* is not about giving. The true giver has no sense of, *"I,"* in anything they do.

So, if you are at a stage of your life where you are not happy and fulfilled, if you can look back a year ago and realize life was better then, it is time to make a change. The essential thing to keep in mind is that change is not about anybody else. Change is about you. Change is not about blaming anyone or anything else. Change needs to be based upon you looking at you. Change needs to be based upon you stop doing things that hurt people or things — even if those things are justified in your own mind. Things that you may have told yourself are right but you know, deep down in inside, that you would not want them done to you. Mostly, change needs to be based upon you being a conduit of giving, not taking. Giving with no sense of self or ego. Giving good and positive things. Giving in silence.

Give it a try. Then, in a year, again take another look at your life. I imagine it will be better.

* * *

14/09/15 20:57

If you have hurt anyone you have hurt yourself.

That's what karma is.

*   *   *

14/09/15 20:56

You can believe whatever you want to be believe but that doesn't make it the truth.

* * *

14/09/15 20:53

If you buy something, use it, and then return it, you are stealing.

What is the karma for stealing?

* * *

14/09/15 20:52

Nothing erases the past.

*   *   *

14/09/15 20:52

How many people you have helped is always overshadowed by how many people you have hurt.

* * *

14/09/15 20:51

You can deny your actions, you can justify what you have done — your friends and your family can support your deeds but if what you have set in motion damages the life of another person then you are the source of that destruction and no words or rationalizations can save you from what will eventually befall you.

* * *

14/09/15 20:50

What happens if no one believed in God?

* * *

14/09/15 20:50

No matter what your motivation, if what you are doing is hurting someone/anyone, what you are doing is wrong.

* * *

14/09/15 20:49

What you have done is what you have done and there is nothing that you can do to change that fact.

* * *

14/09/15 20:49

Most of the things people say are not based upon the truth, they are based upon wanting other people to believe what they believe.

* * *

14/09/15 20:48

You project your own definitions onto the words you read.

*   *   *

14/09/15 20:48

When you continually blame everyone but yourself, who do you think is really at fault?

*   *   *

14/09/15 20:47

Why do you believe what that person is saying?

* * *

14/09/15 20:47

If you look for the bad in everyone, everyone will look for the bad in you.

*   *   *

14/09/15 20:46

How many things would you have never thought about if the idea had not been planted in your brain by someone else?

* * *

14/09/15 20:45

Why do you expect that anyone should do anything for you?

*   *   *

14/09/15 20:45

When you criticize somebody, the only person you make look bad is yourself.

*   *   *

14/09/15 20:44

Can you admit that you are the one at fault?

* * *

14/09/15 20:44

Is your life an interpretation of reality or is it true reality?

* * *

14/09/15 20:43

Going for broke generally leaves you broke.

* * *

14/09/15 20:42

Many people must justify what they have done and why they have done it.

If you must explain your actions, those actions are wrong.

Right action is obvious and needs no explanation.

* * *

14/09/15 20:41

If you are the only person telling other people who and what you are that means that you are the only person believing it.

The truly accomplished person says nothing because everyone already knows what they have achieved.

* * *

14/09/15 20:40

You can claim to be anything that you want to be but that does not make your claim the truth.

* * *

14/09/15 20:39

Once you know how to do it, you know how to do it.

* * *

14/09/15 20:39

Saying, *"I am sorry,"* and meaning it, is one of the most sacred human expressions.

*   *   *

14/09/15 20:38

Everything <u>is</u> your fault.

* * *   14/09/15 20:37

Your life is defined by three things:

    what you do,

    what you do to others,

    and what others do to you.

What do you do?

What do you do to others?

If you hurt anyone, at any time, for any reason, what do you think you will encounter in life?

*   *   *

14/09/15 20:36

Do you try to fix any damage that you have created or do you try to find a reason to justify your actions?

* * *

14/09/15 20:35

Everybody has a reason for doing what they do but most of these reasons are simply excuses.

*   *   *

14/09/15 20:35

There is no going back in time.

*   *   *

14/09/15 20:34

You know what you think you know but you don't know what you don't think you know.

*   *   *

14/09/15 20:34

If you have time to think, you think.

*   *   *

14/09/15 20:29

When you don't have anything better to do you generally do the wrong thing.

* * *

14/09/15 20:28

Are you stating your opinion as a fact?

* * *

14/09/15 20:27

True spirituality begins with you thinking about others first.

Who do you think about?

* * *

14/09/15 20:26

If you have a lot, you can think about what you have. If you have a little you will not think about what you have, you will only think about what you don't have.

*   *   *

14/09/15 20:25

You will never truly understand another person's reality.

* * * 14/09/15 20:24

If it is only in your mind it is only in your mind.

*   *   *

14/09/15 20:23

When you have high expectations life is never going to turn out the way you want it to turn out.

* * *

14/09/15 20:22

If you do a good deed and no one knows about it did you do a good deed at all?

* * *

14/09/15 20:22

Don't you have anything better to do?

*   *   *

14/09/15 20:21

How aware are you of being aware?

The Zen

www.ingramcontent.com/pod-product-compliance
Lightning Source LLC
Chambersburg PA
CBHW071234160426
43196CB00009B/1062